101 TRUMPET TIPS

STUFF ALL THE PROS KNOW AND USE

BY SCOTT BARNARD

ISBN 978-1-61774-120-3

HAL•LEONARD® CORPORATION

7777 W. BLUEMOUND RD. P.O. BOX 13819 MILWAUKEE, WI 53213

In Australia Contact:
Hal Leonard Australia Pty. Ltd.
4 Lentara Court
Cheltenham, Victoria, 3192 Australia
Email: ausadmin@halleonard.com.au

Visit Hal Leonard Online at
www.halleonard.com

ACKNOWLEDGMENTS

Many thanks to Martin Bunce for his help and advice.

Recording credits

Trumpet – Jim Lynch

Sax – Howard McGill

Drums, programming, and mixing – Chris Burgess for redherringaudio.com

Photography by Hannah Hill and Alex Mead

TABLE OF CONTENTS

1 SINGLE TONGUING

In trumpet playing, the vast majority of notes are tongued using a single-tonguing technique, so it makes sense to invest some time in getting this right. The tongue is used to start the note cleanly, at a precise moment. Let's think about the mechanics of this.

Breathe in deeply and hold the air for a moment, place the tip of your tongue behind the top teeth toward the roof of the mouth, as if pronouncing "tu." Then, release the air pressure by drawing the tongue back quickly. Think of this action as a tiny "explosion" to start each note. Try it out on the following exercise; breath marks (ʼ), are suggestions only:

TRACK 1

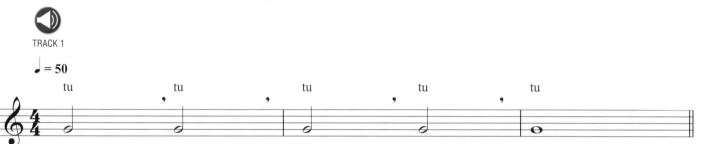

Use a metronome for this exercise, as it will concentrate your efforts in getting the tongue to release at exactly the right moment. Once mastered, it's time to pick up the tempo. Try to do this exercise at the start of every practice session.

TRACK 2

TRACK 3

TRACK 4

TRACK 5

♩ = 80

For this final exercise, try to play it using just one breath. Over time, gradually increase the tempo so that you approach 120 b.p.m. Take the tempo to just over where you are comfortable. The idea here is to make sure that your single tonguing overlaps the speed at which you can double or triple tongue (explained next). In this way, you won't have trouble tonguing at any tempo and you will have a choice of which tonguing technique to use where they overlap.

TRACK 6

♩ = 80-120

Some method books advocate the use of the syllables "ta," "da," or "du" for single tonguing. The "ta" sound works well, but it takes slightly longer to reset the tongue position, so I would advocate "tu." The use of "da" or "du" may be useful if a softer attack is required (see Tip 8).

In the low register, change the syllable to "tor" or "dor." In the high register, use "tee" or "dee." Getting the vowel sound correct for the register helps you to achieve the right air speed.

② DOUBLE TONGUING

There are tempos at which the single-tonguing technique becomes difficult to use; this is where double tonguing comes in handy. It is produced by using the single tongue "tu" followed by a "ku" sound, made by the back of the tongue. This gives the tip of the tongue time to get back in position for another "tu."

Practice the first two exercises on the following page without the trumpet. If you have not tried this before, it may feel quite strange and unlikely to produce good results, but over time, it will improve. Say it loudly.

Now try it with the trumpet. Work on getting the "ku" sound as clear as the "tu" sound.

TRACK 7

TRACK 8

As the "ku" sound becomes more distinct, move on to these exercises:

TRACK 9

TRACK 10

TRACK 11

Your goal is to get the "tu" and "ku" to sound the same; when tonguing at a faster tempo this tends to even out. The suggested metronome marking on the exercise below should ensure that your double tonguing overlaps your single tonguing speed. It may take many months of practice to achieve the faster tempos cleanly.

For the more advanced among you, think about double tonguing with pitch changes and include some intervals. It is common to find double tonguing trickier when descending or in the higher register. In both cases, ensure that you have plenty of air support.

3 TRIPLE TONGUING

Triple tonguing is handy for playing fast triplets and uses the same syllables as double tonguing, but they are arranged in a different order.

There are two ways to do this: either "tu, ku, tu" or "tu, tu, ku." It's a good idea to be fluent with both methods, as both are useful, depending on the context.

When playing a series of triplets, both methods contain two "tu" sounds together:

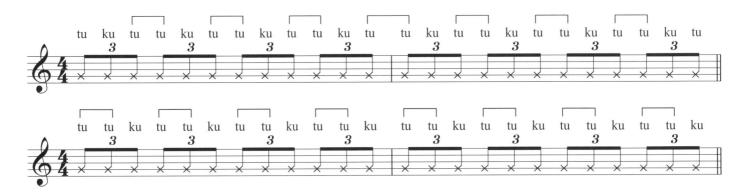

Try using the "tu, ku, tu" approach first, then "tu, tu, ku." Which do you find works the best here?

TRACK 17

TRACK 18

As with double tonguing, your ultimate goal is to be able play them evenly and at tempos that overlap the upper end of your single-tonguing speed.

TRACK 20

Here is an advanced technique; it is similar to passages from *Scheherazade* by Rimsky-Korsakov (although written in a different rhythmic notation here).

Look at the suggested tonguing below the notes. There are many "tu" syllables one after another, which could be very tricky at this tempo. Another approach would be to use the "tu, tu, ku" pattern (shown above the notes) with a "ku" on the single, triplet eighth-notes. Ensure that you accent these single notes to get them to "speak" properly. With this method, there are only two "tu" sounds in succession.

TRACK 21

There are many good books for additional study on all types of tonguing, including the *Arban Cornet Method* and Allen Vizzutti's *Trumpet Method.*

WHAT'S THE TEMPERATURE?

In most playing situations, you have little control over the temperature of the environment you are playing in, but the temperature of your instrument makes a big difference to your intonation. If you have ever done a gig in a church, you will know that they can be quite cold and drafty, also these types of engagements often require you to play nothing for several movements, or you may be waiting for 20 minutes for a bride to walk down the aisle. In these situations (as well as playing outside in cold conditions), your instrument will quickly get cold. This means you will be playing flat. If you try to play when the trumpet is cold, you will find that you tire very quickly, as you will need to lip every note to stay vaguely in tune. To avoid this, blow some air through your instrument in any long rest periods.

Playing in very hot conditions will have the opposite effect—you will be playing sharp. This is harder to control, but if you have a choice, try to keep out of strong sunlight. You may also need to pull out your tuning slide a little.

So remember: cold = flat, hot = sharp.

WHY WARM UP?

There are two reasons to warm up. First, you need to center your concentration—getting "in the zone," if you like. Second, you need to prepare physically for what you are about to ask you body to do—in much the same way as an athlete would.

A warm up can last from 5 to 20 minutes, depending on your level of playing. It's a good idea to start your practice session an hour or so after your warm up, if time allows. The warm up allows you to focus on the fundamentals of trumpet playing, one element at a time. These are:

- **Buzzing on the mouthpiece** – try to use as little pressure as possible and ensure that the buzz is focused in the center. Your goal is to get the buzz to sound as pure as possible (i.e., not an airy sound). Practice buzzing long tones, scales, and arpeggios (see Tip 6).

- **Tonguing** – you can use some of the single-tonguing exercises (Tip 1), on varying pitches, to perfect your articulation.

- **Breathing** – play long, easy notes while listening to your tone. Think about your diaphragm and producing a steady stream of fast-moving air.

- **Fingers** – work on getting your fingers perfectly coordinated with your tongue.

THE BUZZ

The "buzz" is probably the most important aspect of brass playing to consider. The quality of sound and range that you are able to achieve on the trumpet is directly related to the quality and range of your buzz. So include some buzzing every day in your practice routine (as suggested in Tip 5). If you don't have the time to practice one day, buzzing can even be done when you are away from your trumpet, perhaps during a car journey or waiting for a bus. How do you make a buzz?

Different notes are produced by buzzing the center of the lips together (not the whole lip area), while muscles at the corners of your mouth (*modiolus*) hold the lips in tension and stop the lips from being separated by fast-moving air. Of course, there are many more facial muscles involved in forming an embouchure, but the *modioli* are the ones that we have more conscious control over.

In a mirror, practice buzzing without your mouthpiece. Take a deep breath and buzz, maintaining a steady airstream. Think about getting the buzz as pure as possible—you don't want any overtones or an airy sound—focus on the center of your lips. Now, change the pitch to a slightly higher one by just adjusting the tension on the corners of your mouth. Continue this up a scale until the corners of your lips begin to tire.

Have a few minutes rest and then try the exercise again with your mouthpiece. Hold it lightly between your thumb and ring finger; in this way you will avoid the temptation to push it against your lips to produce higher pitches.

It's important to remember that it is the vibration of the lips that achieves a given pitch. The upper register is obtained by a faster buzz, involving more air and therefore more tension at the corners of the mouth to hold it all in balance. Many players fail when they try to play higher by pressing the mouthpiece harder against the lips. This will achieve a higher note (as it will put the lips in greater tension), but not for long. If you use a lot of mouthpiece pressure, the blood circulation in the lips will be cut off, resulting in no buzz at all and possible bruising.

A fun exercise to try is the "siren." Using just the mouthpiece, buzz a low pitch, then play a glissando upwards to the highest pitch that you can, and back down again. A glissando is a continuous slide in pitch (see Tip 24).

Buzzing, if practiced regularly, can dramatically improve your tone, range, and endurance.

The strength of your embouchure is something that improves over time, given regular practice in this area.Using the buzzing exercises from Tip 6 on a daily basis will help a great deal to strengthen your embouchure in a controlled way, as will the following exercise.

Long notes – by holding a note for a long time, your embouchure will work harder and increased strength will be achieved. Try the following exercises. Always take a good breath and make sure that you are not using excessive mouthpiece pressure.

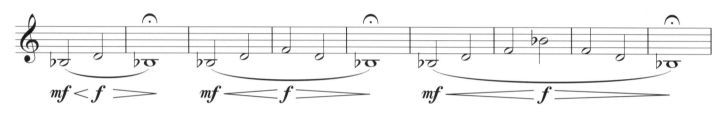

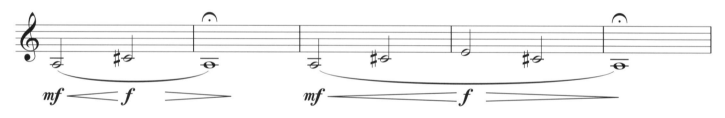

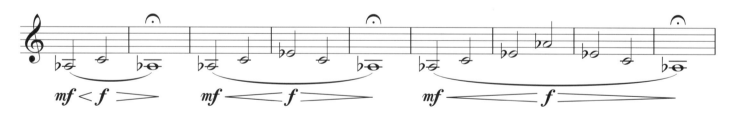

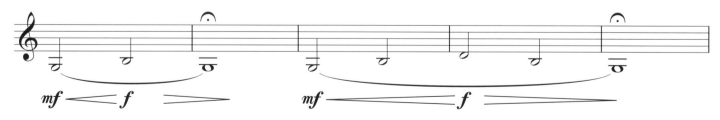

You can vary this exercise by using a dominant seventh, minor, or diminished seventh chord. Lip flexibility exercises are another good way to increase embouchure strength, as described in Tip 14.

8 LEGATO TONGUING

Legato indicates that musical notes are played or sung smoothly and connected. To play in a legato way, you need to think of using a slightly different tonguing technique. With single tonguing, we discussed using the syllable "tu." For a legato effect, change it to "du"; this is also known as "soft" tonguing. The "du" syllable can be used for playing smoothly as well as helping you to achieve a difficult slur—perhaps to a high note or over a wide interval.

TRACK 22

9 WHAT COMES IN...

If you've ever watched a baby sleeping, you may have noticed that its stomach expands and contracts—it is using its diaphragm correctly. We all start off breathing in this way, but somehow over the years we end up breathing high up in our chests. To play a brass instrument properly, you will need to train yourself to breathe like a baby again. When you use your diaphragm, you will be able to have access to a far greater supply of air and have better control over it. This means that your notes will have enough volume, be supported (producing a bright, full tone), and you'll have a greater degree of finesse over your dynamic range. So how does it work?

Breathing in – when you breathe in (always through your mouth), the diaphragm (a strong sheet of muscle below the lungs) and the intercostals (muscles between the ribs) contract downwards, this causes a vacuum in the chest cavity and air to rush into the lungs.

Breathing out – when you breathe out, the diaphragm returns to its natural resting position and so pushes air out. Use your diaphragm to regulate the intensity of the exhalation.

How do I know if my diaphragm is working?

Stand about six inches from a wall. Place a small piece of paper against it. Take a full breath, and then try to hold the paper against the wall using only your breath. To do this you will need to keep the air pressure up using your diaphragm, and refine the air stream by making it pass through a smaller area between your lips. How far away can you stand and still accomplish this? Can you feel the extra work it takes when your lungs are becoming empty?

Repeat this exercise, and over a few weeks, lengthen both the breathing in and out durations (this will increase your air capacity). Try to get the same feeling when playing the trumpet. Eventually (once you're breathing like a baby!), you will do this automatically and only have to remind yourself now and again.

10 PROJECTION

What is projection? Well, it's simply being able to be heard over a distance, like an opera singer being heard over a large orchestra, even at the back of the room. How can this be achieved? There are many things that need to come together in order to have good projection:

- A professional quality instrument is a great starting point, as it will have a good resonance and the potential to carry your sound over a long distance.

- A focused tone is essential, otherwise your sound will dissipate easily. Use the buzzing exercises to work on this aspect.

- Excellent air-stream support is essential.

- Your bell should be up; if you point your trumpet at the floor, your sound will not travel.

- Aim your sound at the very back of the auditorium. You can pick a spot before the audience arrives.

- You must practice in this way at home. See Tip 41. If you leave it until the performance, you'll find that you are working much harder than normal and you'll be lucky to make it to intermission.

11 JOIN THE DOTS

It's important to remember that the notation a composer has written is only a guide. Your job is to bring it to life. Play the following phrase:

It's a challenge to make an easy melody like this sound interesting. But, you may have noticed that the great players seem to make even the simplest phrases sound great. Obviously a great tone, articulation, and a sense of time all help, but there is another concept that you might find useful. Look at the next example, but this time sing it.

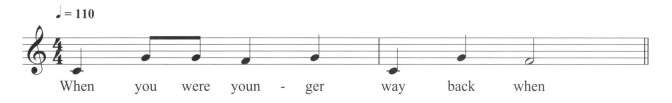

When   you   were   youn - ger   way   back   when

Now play the example again, in exactly the same way in which you sang it. Hopefully you noticed a difference?

You should discover that when you sang it, it became more of a musical sentence and it had more of a direction and sense of purpose. You may have accented some notes more than others, to draw attention to some of the words. Think of these musical sentences as one continuous stream of air and your tongue "slicing" it up to produce a little clarity on each note.

12 THE RIGHT HAND

To get a relaxed valve-playing action, it's important to remember that only the left hand holds the trumpet in position—the right hand is not needed for this and should only be used for the valves. Make sure that the valves are being pressed down straight and not to one side, as this will result in valve wear and sticky valves.

Correct right-hand position

To ensure that your right-hand fingers stay in the correct position, place your right-hand thumb in between the 1st and 2nd valve casing, under the lead pipe. Do not place your little finger in the finger hook (see Tip 75) and keep your hand relaxed.

13 NO TONGUE

When playing normally you would begin a note with the tongue. As an exercise, try playing separate notes up and down a scale without using the tongue. This will help you to get each buzz starting immediately and encourage you to use plenty of air support. (This technique is rarely used in a performance though.)

 **FLEXIBILITY**

The ability to slur smoothly and accurately between notes is essential for good trumpet playing. Flexibility exercises will develop this, and when practiced consistently, are a sure way to build up stamina.

Play all of the following exercises with a metronome to ensure that the pitches change at exactly the right moment. Extend the exercises by following the same patterns, but with different valves. Try valves 2, 1, 1 & 2, 2 & 3, 1 & 3, and 1, 2 & 3.

TRACK 23

Slur Control

When slurring from one note to another, several things need to happen at the same time for a smooth result:

- **Buzz speed** – the corners of the lips tighten for higher notes

- **Vowel change** – middle register notes should be played while forming the syllable "ahh," and higher notes with an "ehh" shape. The previous exercise would therefore be "ahh, ehh, ahh, ehh, ahh."

- **Air support change** – when slurring upwards, a little more air support is needed at the same time as the vowel change

- **Mouthpiece pressure** – there should be no change in mouthpiece pressure. Only use the points above.

Try the same exercise again, but this time sing it with the vowel changes and air support changes. Then play it with the trumpet while thinking about these points.

Try this next exercise:

TRACK 24

How did it sound? Chances are that you caught a G slightly on your way up to the higher C. To avoid this, imagine a pigeon hole rack, the sort they might use in a mail room.

Here's the harmonic series starting with the lowest note at the bottom of the "rack" (see Tip 31 for a notated version):

Valves:	Open	2	1	1 & 2	2 & 3	1 & 3	1, 2 & 3
	C	B	B♭	A	A♭	G	F♯
	B♭	A	A♭	G	G♭	F	E
	G	F♯	F	E	E♭	D	C♯
	E	D♯	D	C♯	C	B	A♯
	C	B	B♭	A	A♭	G	F♯
	G	F♯	F	E	E♭	D	C♯
	C	B	B♭	A	A♭	G	F♯

Play the last exercise again, but this time think of the pigeon hole rack, and "post" the higher C in the correct compartment, without falling into the "G" slot. Once you've perfected this, it will mean that all of the "Slur Control" points are happening simultaneously. Now try these more advanced flexibility exercises:

For further flexibility exercises, I would recommend *How Brass Players Do It*, by John Ridgeon.

50-50

In an ideal world, we would all be walking around with Hollywood smiles, sporting perfectly straight teeth. The real world is not always like that! Most teachers will advocate placing the mouthpiece centrally on the lips. This is a good approach, as it means the embouchure muscles are being used evenly.

Some may find that, due to slightly uneven teeth, a central position is not comfortable, and moving the mouthpiece very slightly to one side may be more suitable. The key thing to remember is that the muscles on both sides of the embouchure need to be involved equally, or 50–50.

However, I have seen students with straight teeth who play way over to one side due to a bad habit. This should be corrected as much as possible. It will take many months of diligent work using a mirror to improve this, but with a more central mouthpiece position, all aspects of trumpet playing will progress, i.e., tone, flexibility, stamina, and range.

The other point to remember is that both lips need to vibrate to produce a good sound. Make sure that the mouthpiece is positioned so that you use an equal amount of top and bottom lip, or 50–50.

CLEAN ON THE INSIDE

Through normal playing, a buildup of debris will occur inside your instrument. You will need to clean your trumpet from time to time to rectify this. The reason for cleaning the inside of your instrument, apart from stopping potentially nasty bacteria from forming, is that the buildup will affect your tone. In extreme cases it will actually make the bore size smaller, resulting in a sharper pitch.

As your trumpet is not dishwasher proof, you will need to use a bathtub or large sink. Add enough luke warm water to cover the bell and a few drops of mild detergent. If the water is too hot, you will strip the lacquer away. Disassemble your instrument, including all slides, and place it in the bath. Let it enjoy a soak for 20 minutes or so. Make sure that you take out the valves, but don't put these in the water— valve cleaning is covered in Tip 18.

Then, use a pull through "snake" to shift any dirt that still remains, and rinse thoroughly with cold water. Dry your instrument and reassemble.

17 SLIDE CLEANING

Most trumpets have four slides, one for each of the valves and a tuning slide. To keep them in optimum condition, a little work is needed now and again.

First, make sure that they are clean on the inside, as described in Tip 16. Then, clean the sliding (un-lacquered) section with metal polish (if used on the lacquered part it will strip it away). Only use the smallest amount necessary to clean off the dirt and any tarnishing. Now polish this all off, hopefully leaving a shiny result. The last step is to add a small amount of "tuning slide and cork grease." This can be obtained from most music stores. Use the correct product, rather than a substitution, as it has the right viscosity and the bottle will last for years. Work the slide back and forth a few times, and you're done!

If the 1st and 3rd trigger slides are a bit stiff using this method, you can loosen them up by adding a few drops of valve oil.

18 VALVE CLEANING

Every trumpet player wants fast valves that never stick. Before carrying out this next tip, make sure that the instrument is clean on the inside (see Tip 16). This is important because loose dirt from the lead pipe can easily enter the valve casing, causing them to stick.

1. Carefully take out one of your valves and place it somewhere safe (do this one at a time if your valves and/or valve casings aren't numbered). Take off the valve end-cap and thread a lint-free cloth (such as a handkerchief) through the casing to remove any dirty oil.

2. Next, thoroughly wipe the valve with the same cloth, making sure that you clean through the valve holes as well. You can then reassemble the valves and apply some valve oil. Do not use any other kind of oil, as it is unlikely to be the correct viscosity.

This next step should be done only when a sticky valve problem occurs:

3. Apply the smallest amount of metal polish to the valve surface and rub gently three of four times, then take off the polish. Make sure that all of the polish has been removed; otherwise it will wear the valve casing. (If you use too much polish, rub too hard, or perform this step too regularly, you may damage the surface of your valves.) Then reassemble the valve and add valve oil.

If this does not fix your sticky valve, you can perform the next step, but if done excessively or for too long, damage may occur to the valves. If you are gentle and use common sense, there should be no problem. However, if you are at all concerned, consult a specialist brass instrument repair center.

4. Perform steps 1–3 but do not remove or rub in the metal polish. Instead, place the valve back in the correct casing and work it up and down a few times (don't force it). Then clean off the polish from the valve and inside casing. Be extra careful to make sure that it is completely removed. Apply some valve oil, and it should be working nicely. If the sticky valve problem persists, see a repair specialist.

19 REPAIRS

Finding a friendly, local brass instrument repair specialist is a must for any serious player. No matter how careful you are, at some point you're likely to get the odd dent. If these are in any of the slides, it will affect your tuning, and therefore needs to be rectified.

Repairs are often much cheaper than you would first think and certainly preferable to buying a new instrument. As well as dent removal, a skilled repairer can correct:

- Persistently sticking valves (not corrected by Tip 18)

- Lost or worn springs for water keys, and corks

- Re-lacquering or re-plating—this can transform your trumpet to like new

- Re-soldering of joints

- Removal of a stuck mouthpiece (to avoid this in the first place, gently screw it in clockwise and remove in the opposite direction)

- Straightening a crumpled bell (using a trumpet stand will stop you from accidently sitting on it!)

20 LOST YOUR BOUNCE?

Over time, valve springs can lose their tension, making the valve slow to return to its resting position. This causes notes to sound "smeared" and fast passages to become more difficult. Also, you may find that the springs have become misshapen, in which case you can replace them. Consult a repair specialist to find out what will work best for you and your instrument.

21 FLUTTER TONGUING

Flutter tonguing is an effect that is widely used in jazz music as well as some contemporary orchestral pieces.It is denoted by the indication "flutter tongue," "flutter," "flt." or "flz.," often with three slashes through the stem of the note (like a tremolo, see Tip 22).

To produce this effect, simply "roll" your "r's" as you play a note. If you have difficulty with this, then bend the tip of your tongue up slightly, so that it is just below the roof of your mouth. Tense the tongue, but not the tip, this needs to be free to vibrate against the roof of your mouth. Now breathe out quickly. If your tongue is close enough to the roof of your mouth it should start to vibrate. Have a listen to the audio track (notated on the following page) to hear how it should sound.

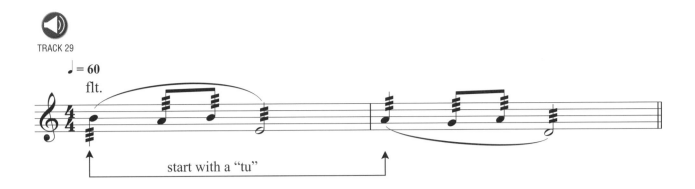

Points to bear in mind are that it is much trickier to flutter tongue in the higher register. Use a "normal" tonguing action to start the note, and keep a well-supported air stream going.

22 TREMOLO

This effect is notated in a similar way to the flutter tongue, except the word "tremolo" or "trem." should appear. Unlike the flutter tongue, the tremolo does not use the tongue to supply the Flamenco guitar-like effect, instead it relies on alternate fingerings (see Tip 31).

Play the note with the normal fingering, then alternate it (very quickly) with an alternate fingering. Remember to keep the air going. It should produce a shimmering quality (as demonstrated on the audio track).

TRACK 30

HALF VALVE

This fun effect is easy to pull off and can add a touch of authenticity to any jazzy solo or phrase. The half-valve technique can be used to create vocal-like sounds, such as those used by Miles Davis, and is frequently employed to "squeeze the juice" out of a note. It is usually denoted by the text "1/2 valve."

You can get different variations of sound depending on how far the valve is pressed down and by how many valves you use. Try this next exercise and experiment with different fingerings to see what produces the best result. The first 12 bars concentrate on the half-valve effect, and the second 12 bars include some new techniques based on the tips covered so far. Track 31 is the demonstration version and track 32 is a backing track for you to have a go.

TRACK 31   TRACK 32
                  Backing Track

24 THE GLISSANDO

The glissando is most often referred to as a "gliss" outside the classical realm, and is best approached by first learning the "rip" (a special effect in its own right). Unlike the human voice, stringed instruments, and trombone, the trumpet can't easily slide between two notes that are a large distance apart; instead, we have to simulate it. The first step in doing this is by working on the rip.

The Rip

Play an A♭ then quickly lip slur up to a high A♭. When you do this, make sure that you're pumping plenty of air through and, as you tighten your embouchure, change your tongue position from "ah" to "eh." You should find that all the harmonics between the two A♭s are produced.

TRACK 33

While keeping the 2nd and 3rd valves down, try the exercise again, but this time after the first note, slightly depress the 1st valve. Make sure the 1st valve is fully up for the final note.

TRACK 34

The Gliss

What you have just played was a half-valve gliss and would be written as below. The gliss can be notated with a straight or wavy line and sometimes the word "gliss." is also added (often with a period to indicate it is an abbreviation).

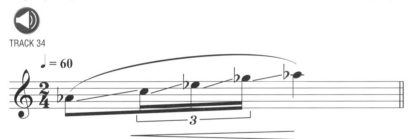

If the start and end notes of the gliss are on different valves, you could use alternate fingerings (see Tip 31), or try the following approach:

Start the gliss shown below with the 2nd valve. When you want to slide, imagine that your first and second fingers are on a seesaw—as you slowly bring up the second finger, the first finger is pressed down. The trick is to time it so that your 2nd valve is fully up and your 1st valve is fully down by the end note.

TRACK 35

Glisses can also be played in a downward direction, as shown in this showbiz-style ending. For this gliss, keep the 1st valve down and add some half-valve action from the 2nd and 3rd valves.

TRACK 36

25 FALLS

Used extensively in jazz and commercial music, the fall is probably one of the most enjoyable effects to play. It is denoted by a downward curved, straight, or wavy line after a note. The fall can vary in length from a "short fall" (perhaps only a step or so) to a "long fall" (often over an octave or more). Arrangers frequently state whether they require a short or long fall.

All falls involve playing a note while loosening the embouchure. To get a transition between the notes, you can use various techniques such as:

- "ripping" down through the harmonic series
- waggling the valves
- using half valves (see Tip 23)—you can start with one valve and gradually add more as you get lower
- any combination of these

How you execute a fall will depend on the context and, therefore, is a matter of taste. Listen to these different versions of falls.

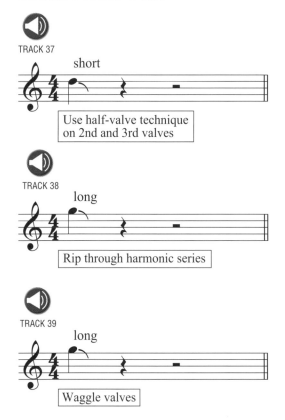

TRACK 37

short

Use half-valve technique on 2nd and 3rd valves

TRACK 38

long

Rip through harmonic series

TRACK 39

long

Waggle valves

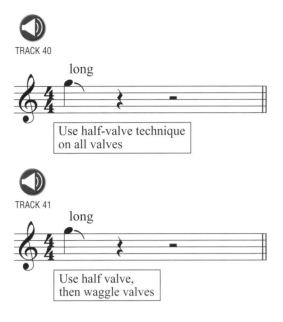

long

Use half-valve technique
on all valves

long

Use half valve,
then waggle valves

26 BENDS

Bends can be used to add a bluesy character to a solo and can be found in soli writing too. The bend is indicated by a small curved line above the staff; sometimes the word "bend" will also be shown. To carry out this effect, you need to drop your jaw very slightly and produce a lower buzz, about a half step below the original note.

Try this exercise on just the mouthpiece to begin with:

Then try to bend the note down and back up by using the technique above.

Here's an example in a bluesy context:

Swing ♩ = 114

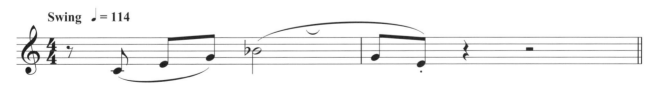

27 DOITS

Another jazz effect is the "doit," signified by an upward curved line, often with the word "doit" written. It's a fast upward glissando using the half-valve technique. The name of the effect is a big clue in helping you to produce it. Your tongue should be forming the word "doit" (pronounced doy-it); by doing this, it changes the cavity in your mouth from an open "o" shape to the smaller "i" shape.

How far you gliss will depend on your range; about an octave is usual. As you go up, use plenty of air. Listen to how it sounds.

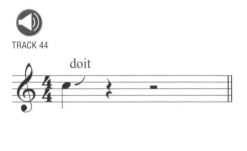

TRACK 44

28 VIBRATO

When playing a phrase (especially a solo line), your aim should be to convey a lyrical quality. One of the best ways to do this is with vibrato. When playing with vibrato, you are varying the pitch a little to create an oscillating effect. There are several ways to do this:

- **Hand vibrato** – this method requires you to move the trumpet on and off the embouchure with the right hand. However, it could lead to some bad habits with mouthpiece pressure and can be very tiring, so it is best avoided.

- **Diaphragm/breath vibrato** – this is achieved by varying the pressure of air, much as a flautist would do. But on a brass instrument, this is harder to control for this purpose and so is rarely used.

- **Lip/jaw vibrato** – this method is more widely used and is very controllable. The pitch variation is made by changing the pitch of the buzz up and down a small amount; this is helped by moving the jaw up and down very slightly at the same time.

A vibrato can be fast or slow, wide or narrow. Always remember that vibrato should be used with taste, such as to make a note "live," or to "warm it up," or convey emotion. However, if overdone, it can sound vulgar. If an arranger does want an exaggerated effect, they will write "vib" or perhaps "Mariachi" to convey the very wide trumpet vibrato of a Mariachi-style band.

A nice way to use vibrato is to gradually add more to a note, to "warm it up." Listen to the long notes on track 45. In the notation, the notes with slashes for noteheads have been added to show where a change in vibrato is happening.

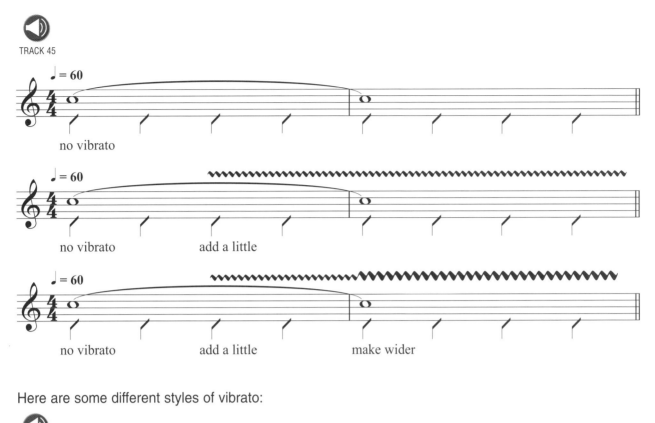

Here are some different styles of vibrato:

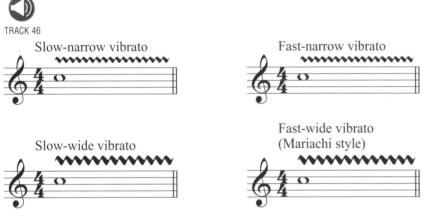

Listen to this last example, a transposed excerpt from *Don Carlo* by Verdi, to spot where the vibrato has been used.

 TRILLS

Certain trills are trickier to play than others. Especially in the higher register (where the harmonic series is closer together), unwanted random notes can creep in. Here's an example of what can happen:

Notated   Should sound like   Often sounds like

To keep this random element at bay, think of buzzing a pitch that is in between the two notes of the trill—in this case C♯. Try trilling from C to D with this thought in mind and see if it improves.

30 LIP TRILLS

Lip trills were the only type of trills available to the natural trumpeters (no valves) of the Baroque era. Nowadays, we can choose to use it as an effect, or to avoid trilling between impossible valve combinations.

Lip trills are very quick lip slurs between two notes. They are executed by rapidly changing the tongue position from "ah" to "ee" and using a fast, well-supported air stream. This is easier to achieve on the higher notes, where the harmonic series is closer together. By using more valves to play the note you're trilling on (see Tip 31), you will make the partials even closer together. For example, if lip slurring upward from a G above the staff, the next partial in the harmonic series is a B♭. If you use the 1st and 3rd valves instead of open, the next partial is an A.

Most trills in jazz music are intended to be lip trills (unless the piece has some classical elements). They may be written as a conventional trill, or just with a wavy line. Sometimes the word "shake" is also given. Here are some preparatory exercises:

TRACK 48

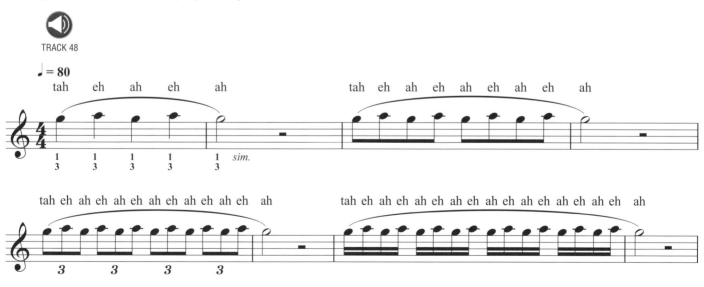

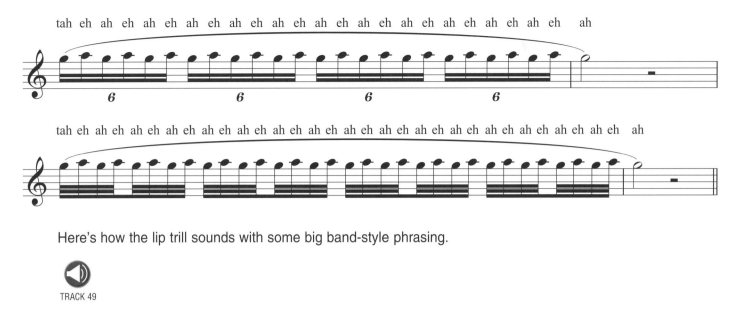

tah eh ah eh ah eh ah eh ah eh ah eh ah eh ah eh ah eh ah eh ah eh ah eh ah eh   ah

Here's how the lip trill sounds with some big band-style phrasing.

TRACK 49

31 ALTERNATE FINGERINGS

Having an alternate fingering that you can use to produce the same pitch is very handy on the trumpet, here are a few reasons why:

- If you find that your trumpet is slightly out of tune for a particular note, an alternate fingering may be better in tune.

- If you are playing a fast passage (or trills) with difficult fingerings, it may be easier to replace one or two of them with alternate fingerings.

- The tremolo effect (see Tip 22) makes use of alternate fingerings.

- Certain lip trills (see Tip 30) will be made easier using alternate fingerings.

So what are these alternate fingerings?

Each valve combination adds a different length of tubing to the trumpet's natural length:

- 2nd valve = half step

- 1st valve = one step

- 1st and 2nd valves = one and a half steps

- 3rd valve = one and a half steps

- 2nd and 3rd valves = two steps

- 1st and 3rd valves = two and a half steps

- 1st, 2nd, and 3rd valves = three steps

From this, we can immediately see that any note played with the 1st and 2nd valves could also be played with just the 3rd valve. This is the only "direct swap" of this nature, but there is another way to produce the same note with different valve combinations. Below is the harmonic series (the notes available for each valve combination) up to the 7th partial for B♭ trumpet. The notes in parentheses indicate notes that are possible; these are the notes that we can use as alternate fingerings. Some of the alternate fingerings are likely to be out of tune to a greater or lesser degree, but for the most part this will be fine if used for the reasons previously mentioned (trills or tremolos).

Harmonic Series

32 TRANSPOSING

Many young trumpet players groan at the suggestion of transposing. Why should we bother learning how to do it? Well, there are some very sound reasons for this:

- Any aspiring orchestral trumpet player will need to transpose. Many popular works are written for trumpet in different keys, often changing between different transpositions in the same piece.

- If you're on a church gig, the organist may thrust a hymn in front of you, mid-service, and ask you to play the descant line.

- You could be in a recording studio and the producer asks you to play the violin part on the trumpet.

- You could be doing a show, the oboe player hasn't turned up, and the whole show begins with an important oboe solo and the director asks you to cover it.

- You may be asked to do some teaching that includes French horn and trombone students.

- Your usual vocalist might be unavailable, and the replacement vocalist needs the arrangement a step lower.

The list could go on!

How is transposition done? Well, if you haven't worked on this before, I would suggest starting with transposing up one step. This is the most useful transposition for a B♭ trumpet as it allows you to play "concert pitch" parts. "Concert pitch" instruments do not transpose, some of which are the C trumpet, violin, flute, oboe, piano, tuned percussion, voice, and the guitar (although the guitar sounds an octave lower than written).

There are two methods that you can combine when transposing, the first involves spotting patterns.

Transposing – Patterns

Play this next exercise.

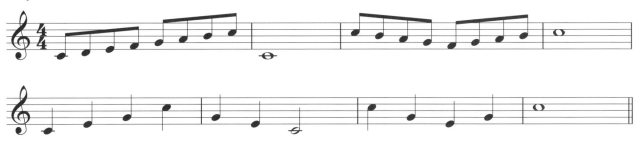

It's unlikely that you read every note; hopefully you realized that there were some familiar patterns. If you didn't, here's what they were:

Now play these same patterns in the key of D major, using the text prompts as a guide. By doing this, you are transposing up a step (this is the same procedure that you would use for playing a part written for trumpet in C, or any concert pitch part). You also mentally "add" a key signature, in this case the key signature of D major.

I haven't written out the transposed version of these next patterns, as I want you to work it out rather than read it. Let's step it up a gear! Play these patterns as written and then transpose them up a step. Remember to add a mental key signature.

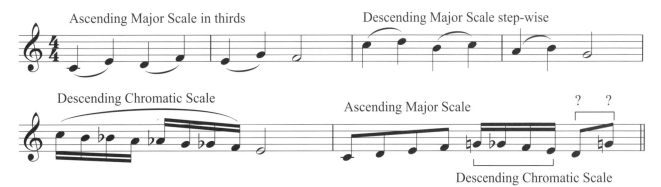

Okay, so what about the last two notes? They don't fit into a clear pattern do they? Well, you could think of them as being the 2nd and 5th degree of the major scale, but a better option is to know what D or G is when transposed up a step. This moves us on to the second transposing method—intervals.

Transposing – Intervals

Here is a chromatic scale with its corresponding transposition:

Concert Pitch (Trumpet in C)	A	A♯/B♭	B	C	C♯/D♭	D	D♯/E♭	E	F	F♯/G♭	G	G♯/A♭
Up One Step (Trumpet in B♭)	B	C	C♯/D♭	D	D♯/E♭	E	F	F♯/G♭	G	G♯/A♭	A	A♯/B♭

By looking at our table, we can see that a D will become an E, and a G will become an A. Now play the previous exercise again, up one step, and include the last two notes this time.

If you have trouble memorizing the above table, cut out 12 squares of paper and write a note name on one side, labeled "Trumpet in C" and the Trumpet in B♭ version on the other side, like this:

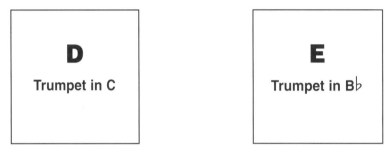

Then mix them up, keeping all the "Trumpet in C" versions face-up, and test yourself. Over time these will become second nature to you.

Transposing – Patterns & Intervals

When you combine these two methods, you'll find that transposition becomes less taxing. On these next excerpts (from *Suite Française*, by Poulenc), spot the patterns and just think about the transpositions for the notes at the beginning and ends of the pattern, plus any notes that don't fit into a pattern. As before, transpose this example up a step (the key signature will be D major). The tempo markings are just to let you know the intended speeds, but take it much more slowly to begin with.

Here are some more excerpts from the same work. This time they're in F major, so your new key signature will be G major. Again, take them at a speed that suits you.

Find as much music as you can to transpose, perhaps a book of hymns or jazz standards. Make sure that it's not too high, as that's not the skill you are working on here. There are many other transpositions that are useful to learn; I would strongly recommend *Vingt-Quatre Vocalises*, by M. Bordogni for further study in this area.

 MUTES

There are many times when you're required to use some sort of mute, but do you ever practice with one? Probably not. It's worth doing occasionally as mutes often add resistance to the trumpet, which will make slurs more difficult, so you may have to blow harder in general. Also, they can make your trumpet out of tune, especially in the lower register, so experiment with a tuner to see which notes need to be lipped in tune.

Here are some of the most common mutes:

(left to right) Plunger, Glenn Miller plunger, Cup, Harmon (wah-wah),
Straight, Bucket, Practice

And some of the more unusual:

(left to right) Pixie, Solotone (clear tone), Derby (hat)

 # 34 THE PLUNGER

One of the most dramatic ways that you can change your sound is by using a plunger mute. You can create a great variety of vocal-like qualities, especially when combined with effects.

There are two basic positions for the plunger: open (held away from the bell) and closed (held over the bell, but with a small gap).

Plunger – open position

Plunger – closed position

Practice changing between these two positions. The "+" means closed and "o" means open.

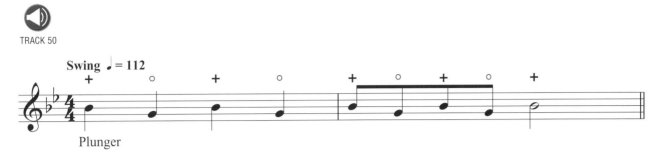

Another way to use a plunger is by changing from closed to open on the same note. The second example produces a wah-wah effect, and if used very fast, can sound like an exaggerated vibrato.

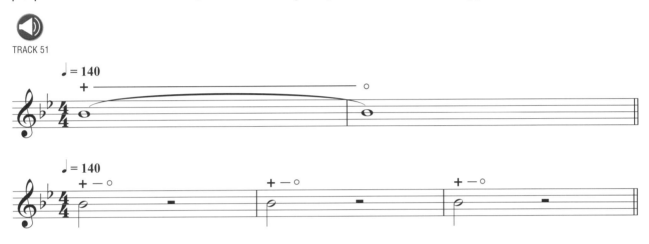

Combining the plunger with other techniques is very effective. In the example below there is a closed plunger with a flutter tongue, a wah-wah effect with a fall, and a closed plunger with a "growl." A growl sounds similar to the flutter tongue, but it is created by making a gargling action with back of the tongue.

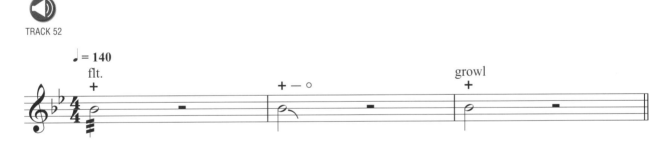

Try all these techniques in the context of a phrase.

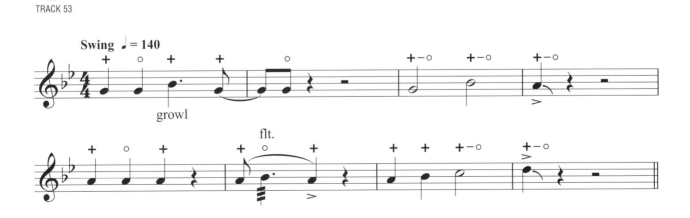

35 PEDAL TONES

Pedal tones are great for warm ups and warm downs as they benefit your playing in several ways:

- They promote you to use a good supply or air, as they are difficult to do without it.

- You can't use too much mouthpiece pressure to play these; the lips need to be free to buzz.

- They encourage the lips to vibrate, causing blood to circulate well.

Drop your jaw slightly lower for each note. You can use all three valves to help with the lowest tones.

TRACK 54

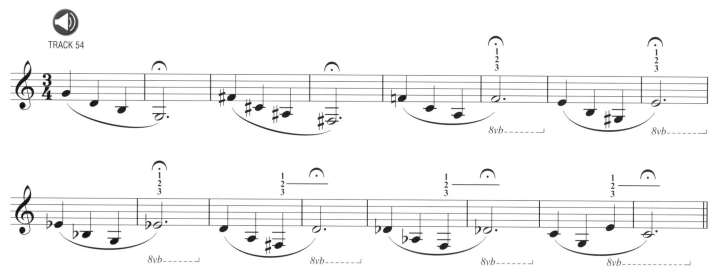

36 ARTICULATION

There are many differences and similarities between classical and jazz music. One of the easiest to trip up on is the interpretation of articulations. Just as in classical music, articulations in jazz can vary slightly from era to era. Below are some broad definitions of the most common:

Articulation	Classical meaning	Jazz meaning
Staccato	Detached (usually half of the written duration)	Detached, slightly fatter
Tenuto	Full value	Fullest value, no separation, slight accent
Accent	Moderately strong attack	Strong attack, full value
Marcato	Strong attack	(Known as a "hat") strong attack and short

Listen to how each of these should sound with a jazz approach.

TRACK 55

The marcato (or "hat") has the greatest difference in jazz, as it is a short note. Have a listen to them in the context of a phrase.

TRACK 56

37 PLAYING WITHIN A GROUP

One of the great joys of playing an instrument is being able to join with others in an ensemble. The trumpet in the wrong hands can be a destructive force if not tempered with good ensemble skills. Here are some points to think about when you play in a group:

- **Listen and be aware** – this should be your natural state. You will have to leave your ego at home! When you're not playing, keep listening to everything else that's happening.

- **Consensus on time** – a group can quickly decide exactly where the beat is in relation to what the conductor is doing, but only if everyone is listening and aware.

- **Balance** – it's crucial to get an ensemble sound. You don't want the sound of an orchestra plus a trumpet. Make sure that your sound blends in with the group. Think of the ensemble having a giant bubble over it, created by a perfect balance. Don't burst through the bubble!

- **Tuning** – listen to how your pitch relates to others. Has the temperature changed causing the wind players to go wildly out of tune?

- **Phrasing** – listen to how others are phrasing, and apply it to your part.

- **Articulations** – match what other players are doing in your section, as well as other sections.

- **Play as one** – just like a swarm of bees or a shoal of fish, the whole ensemble needs to think and "move" as one. If you have ever been a passenger on a motorcycle, you will know that you have to move at the same time as the driver—if you don't, balance suffers, and you'll certainly have troubles in the curves!

- **Overall musical effect** – be aware that your part is one ingredient in the recipe; by combining with the other players, you create the overall effect. The higher goal is the ensemble; make your part contribute to that.

 38 CHOOSING A TEACHER

One teacher can't teach you everything, but hopefully they can teach you something! When choosing a new teacher, have the confidence to ask for a trial lesson. That way, both parties can decide whether they want to continue. By the time you have been playing for a couple of years, if you do not have one already, you will need to find a trumpet specialist (not a specialist on some other instrument). Look for someone who:

- makes you feel relaxed
- is interested in you and your progress
- is happy to take the time to explain how to do things clearly
- is patient
- can see the positives in your playing
- is interested in the trumpet, and music in general
- can demonstrate well, and plays regularly
- is inspiring

The very best of teachers will have all these attributes, plus one more. The aim of every teacher should be to give you the tools to teach yourself. That way, you can solve problems on the trumpet for years to come.

 39 TEACHING THE PROS

As a trumpet player, you are always learning and improving. Even professional players occasionally seek the guidance of a trumpet "guru" from time to time—often from "celebrity" players dropping into town to do a date or two. If you're playing professionally, think about who might inspire you; it doesn't have to be Wynton Marsalis, Maurice André, or Jon Faddis (although those would all make for an interesting afternoon!), but perhaps someone in your area who is at top of their game.

When you book a consultation, make sure that you have a specific goal that you want to achieve, and take some music along. Is it your production that you want to work on? If so, take an example of what you are struggling with. Maybe you're having trouble soloing on a specific set of chords; again, take along the example and a backing track if you have one. In other words, make sure you are getting the most out of your time with them!

 40 SILENT PRACTICE

There are some occasions when you need to practice, but doing so may inconvenience others, such as back stage before a concert. In these situations, a practice mute is a good idea. However, it's not ideal to use one for your regular practice sessions, as you will not be able to work on your tone. Another relatively recent development is the "Silent Brass" system. It can be fun to use, as you can play along with any audio you have and add reverb, which you can use to work on your tuning. However, neither of these options should be a long-term solution, as the resistance is different than playing without them.

If you find that you are using one of these options for your regular practice, then it may be time to re-think things. Could you play in a different part of your home, where it will be less intrusive to others? Alternatively, could you practice at a different time of the day? If the answer is no, you could look for an alternative venue. Perhaps you could approach your local church, college, or community center to see if they have some space they are willing to let you use, or maybe a venue that is unoccupied during the day or evening (depending on what time you want to practice). It may take a while to find the perfect location, but it will be well worth it.

41 SIZE MATTERS

When you play in a large concert hall or venue, you need to project your sound to fill the space (see Tip 10). To be able to project without getting tired, you need to practice in this way (all the time). The trouble is, most of us don't have a very large space to practice in, so we end up playing to the size of the room (i.e., without any projection and at a relatively low volume). When practicing, imagine that you are playing in the largest venue that you've ever performed in or seen a concert at, even if you're just working on technical exercises. This is especially important to do when at a recording studio, where space is often at a premium and there is no sound coming back at you from the sound-insulated walls.

42 LEARNING JAZZ SOLOS

Many players who venture into the world of jazz buy a book of transcribed jazz solos. It's difficult to perfectly transcribe an improvisation, note for note—the end result is often tricky to read and play! Although useful for sight-reading practice, there is much more value in transcribing them for yourself. In this way, the phrasing and musical ideas will sink in far better. Your ultimate goal is to learn from these so that you have a richer palette on which to draw for your own improvisations.

The fastest way to learn a foreign language is to spend some time in a country that speaks that language, that way you immerse yourself in the culture and naturally learn the vocabulary, phrasing, and inflections. You can do the same when learning jazz—listen to the key players that shaped the jazz movement and join some local jazz groups. Find a group where you feel safe enough to try out some improvisation. After a while, you will pick up the rhythms and style, and begin to understand the harmony more easily.

Your jazz vocabulary should include some pentatonic and blues scales, as well as modes. You don't have to learn these all at once—introduce them gradually to your daily practice routine. After some time, it's a good idea to find a specialist jazz teacher, who can help you further your development.

43 BLUES SOLOS

The most common vehicle for the beginning jazz improviser is the 12-bar blues (so called because there are 12 bars that repeat the same sequence of chords). Here is a basic blues progression where each chord lasts for one bar:

I7	IV7	I7	I7
IV7	IV7	I7	I7
V7	IV7	I7	I7 (V7)

The most common key for a blues is F major (concert pitch). This is because all the instruments within an ensemble will be playing in a straightforward key. Concert pitch instruments will be in F major (one flat), B♭ instruments in G major (one sharp), and E♭ instruments in D major (two sharps).

Here is the progression expressed as chord symbols in the key of G:

In a 12-bar blues, there are three, four-bar phrases. Often, these are riff-based. Have a look at this funky blues head:

G7	C7	G7	G7
C7	C7	G7	G7
D7	C7	G7	G7 (D7)

🔊 TRACK 57

Original head
Funk ♩ = 86

You can break the task of improvising into smaller elements. Let's look at two ways in which to improvise on this tune, starting with the rhythm.

In this next example, you can see that I have kept the pitches unchanged, but the rhythm has been altered to create some interest. Notes that have been altered are circled for ease of comparison.

🔊 TRACK 58

Rhythms altered

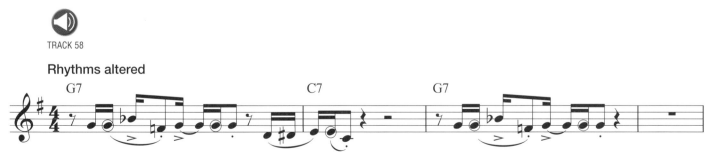

Let us now go back to the original rhythm, but change some of the pitches. Compare this with the original version.

TRACK 59

Pitches altered

Here is a version incorporating both rhythm and pitch variations:

TRACK 60

Rhythms and Pitches altered

Try out some of your own variations using the backing track; approach it in the same way as outlined above. It will last for 48 bars (four choruses of 12 bars each).

TRACK 61
Backing Track – 48 bars

On an instrument like the piano or guitar, when your finger is in the right position for a note, it should sound as you intended it to. On the trumpet, it's not so easy. To play a note in tune, you have to be able to hear it first. If you can't hear it accurately, you are likely to crack it or play it out of tune.

The best way to improve your ear is with sight-singing. Get a hymnbook or some material that you don't already know, and try to sing it. Work on a few bars at a time, checking the pitch with your trumpet afterwards. If you struggle with this, then work on the individual intervals first. Here are some well-known melodies to help you learn them. The first two notes of each melody (unless otherwise stated) form the interval.

Interval	Melody
Minor 2nd	*Jaws* theme
Major 2nd	Doe a Deer (*The Sound of Music*), Frère Jacques, Happy Birthday (2nd & 3rd notes)
Minor 3rd	Axel F, Greensleeves
Major 3rd	Oh When the Saints Go Marching In, Kum Ba Yah
Perfect 4th	Love Me Tender, Amazing Grace, Here Comes the Bride, We Wish You a Merry Christmas
Augmented 4th/ Diminished 5th	The Simpsons theme, Maria (*West Side Story*)
Perfect 5th	Star Wars theme, Jurassic Park theme, Twinkle, Twinkle Little Star (2nd & 3rd notes), Kum Ba Yah (1st & 3rd notes)
Minor 6th	The Entertainer (3rd & 4th notes)
Major 6th	Angels (Robbie Williams), My Bonnie Lies Over the Ocean
Minor 7th	Somewhere (*West Side Story*), original *Star Trek* theme (1st & 3rd notes)
Major 7th	Somewhere Over the Rainbow (1st & 3rd notes)
Octave	Somewhere Over the Rainbow (1st & 2nd notes)

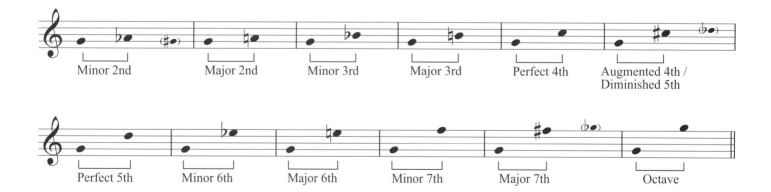

45 POSTURE

Standing or sitting in the correct manner while playing the trumpet is an essential habit to adopt. Your posture can drastically improve or degrade your performance. Try to remember these points:

- If you are sitting, your elbows should never be on your knees or abdomen!

- Keep your back straight, but with minimal tension. This will also make you feel generally more alert.

- The upper and lower jaw should be aligned.

- Keep your head up so that the throat is not constricted and air can flow freely.

- The shoulders should be relaxed.

- Your trumpet should be near to a horizontal position; this will ensure even pressure on both lips. The chest cavity will be easier to expand (proper breathing and support will be better) and projection will be easier as you're not pointing down at the floor.

Standing posture

Sitting posture

46 CHOOSING A PRO INSTRUMENT

Generally, you get what you pay for when purchasing a trumpet. Student models are adequate to a certain level, but at some point, you're going to want to upgrade to something more professional. So, what do you get for your extra bucks? With a professional instrument, you will have better and more resonant materials that have been more carefully put together, with more processes done by hand. The finish will also be of a higher quality, meaning your new trumpet should last years. Additionally, you will have a 1st-valve trigger slide, and other slides and the valves will work more efficiently. A professional instrument should be more in tune, project better, have a more immediate response, and likewise, the potential for an improvement in tone.

There are a growing number of options for professional trumpets these days. You may like the one that your teacher uses, or perhaps you want the same kind that a famous player uses. You should aim to get one that is right for you and the type of playing you expect to be doing (there is little point in buying a trumpet designed for lead trumpet playing if you are likely to be playing in an orchestra). Take your teacher (or a seasoned player) along when trying out a new instrument, and don't forget to take along your own mouthpiece. Also, take a tuner to check that it plays in tune. Many shops will let you take a trumpet "on trial," so take advantage of that if they offer it, and see how it performs in various groups.

47 FINGER EXERCISES

How well your fingers are working will affect the clarity of the starts and ends of your notes. It may seem obvious, but your valves need to be fully depressed (quickly) in order for them to function correctly. The biggest fingering change happens between the 1st and 3rd valves and the 2nd valve, e.g., D to F♯. Try the following exercises and make sure that the valves are synchronizing properly. Playing them slurred will make any imperfections more obvious, but also try them tongued. Use conventional fingerings.

TRACK 62

48 HOW TO REHEARSE

One of the skills of a professional trumpet player is to know how to rehearse properly. Often you will have a rehearsal in the afternoon and a performance in the evening. Unless you have "chops of steel," there is no point in sounding amazing in the rehearsal, only to have no lip left for the concert. In a rehearsal you could leave out some of the higher passages, or play them down an octave. A professional conductor or music director will appreciate that you're saving your lip for the performance.

Church organists need to be handled with care! If they are inexperienced musicians, they may want to run through the pieces repeatedly (for their own practice). This is made worse by the fact that organs are often out of tune, the building can be cold (affecting your tuning, and so adding extra strain), and the pieces are likely to be demanding on your stamina anyway. So, if they want to run pieces more than once, and you are happy with the way in which you played, play your part down an octave or ask if you actually need to play, as you want to save your lip.

49 PARTS OF THE MOUTHPIECE

The mouthpiece is the first thing that can shape your sound, after the buzz. They are usually made from brass and plated with silver, nickel, or gold. To gain a greater understanding of how mouthpieces can vary, let's look at its different parts.

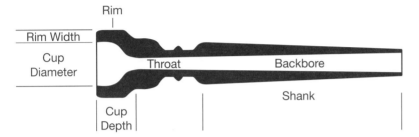

Rim – This is the part that is in contact with your lips.

- A wide rim will be comfortable and aid endurance as a smaller section of the lip is left to buzz. Your endurance may improve, but your tone may suffer if too wide.

- A narrow rim will result in better flexibility, but less endurance (as more lip is involved).

As well as the width, the contour of the rim can vary.

- A flat rim aids endurance; a rounded rim aids flexibility.

- The inner edge of the rim is called the "bite." If it's sharp it will result in notes with a clear attack, but may dig into your lips if you are using too much pressure.

Cup – This is where the tone is generated; it's a resonating chamber.

- If the cup is shallow, it will allow notes to speak quickly and the higher register will be easier.

- If the cup is very shallow, the sound will be thin and the lower register will often be unobtainable.

- If the cup is deep, the lower notes will sound better, but the trade off is that your endurance can suffer and the upper range will be harder to produce.

Throat – If the throat is wide, you can push lots of air through and make a huge sound without distorting it. At softer volumes, it also allows more air to travel through.

Backbore – If this is quite tight, you can get more projection and a brighter sound. Some players get the backbore widened (which most brass repair specialists can do for you). This will result in less resistance and the lower range will feel easier. If too wide, this can lead to endurance issues.

Shank – This is the part that fits into the leadpipe.

There are many different mouthpiece makes and sizes, all with different numbering systems, each made for different applications and players' preferences. Just take a look at this list of players and their mouthpieces (from *www.trumpetplayerprofiles.com*).

Arturo Sandoval	Mt Vernon Bach 3C
Bill Chase	Schilke custom 6a4a mouthpiece
Jon Faddis	Schilke Custom Faddis heavyweight
Maynard Ferguson	Custom Monette mouthpieces
Bobby Shew	Marcinkiewicz and Yamaha custom designed mouthpieces
Lou Soloff	Bach Mt. Vernon 3C with a 25 throat; a Schilke 14A4A
Allen Vizzutti	Signature Marcinkiewicz and Yamaha mouthpieces
Wynton Marsalis	Monette PRANA B2S3 (www.wyntonmarsalis.org)

So, what mouthpiece is right for you? That's a tricky question and depends on:

- what style of music you play
- your endurance levels
- the sound you have now and the sound you want to produce
- your upper and lower register

You shouldn't get a particular model just because someone else uses it, as you are very unlikely to have the same dental and embouchure make-up as them. Ask your teacher for advice and try a few different ones out at a music shop. Give yourself some time to get used to a new mouthpiece and don't switch to a new one on the day of a concert.

50 PRACTICING SANS TRUMPET

It can be beneficial to break up your practice session with some work that doesn't involve your embouchure. In this way, you can give your chops a rest while continuing to improve. One of the ways that you can do this is by practicing the fingerings for scales, as these should ultimately be played using "muscle memory" (once thoroughly learned, fingerings become subconscious).

As an example, play a C major scale with just your fingers while hearing the sound it will make in your head. As well as the fingering, you will be rehearsing "perfect" scales, where there are no poor attacks, mistimed valves, and your tone is even and full; this is a very positive reinforcement technique. Try this with every scale. You can do the same with tricky passages—slow them down in your mind and hear yourself playing them beautifully. You can also do this when you're away from the trumpet completely (sitting at a desk, on a train, in the car, etc.).

51 TOOL KIT

Like a good Boy Scout, it pays to be prepared! You only need a few basic items to keep your trumpet in top condition. These items are a pull-through (snake), mouthpiece brush, valve oil, tuning slide grease, and handkerchief.

(left to right) Pull through (snake), Valve oil, Tuning slide grease, Handkerchief, (front) Mouthpiece brush

In addition to these, you should also carry a pencil and eraser, trumpet stand, and mutes (practice, straight, cup, Harmon, and possibly a plunger and bucket mute).

(back, left to right) Practice, Cup, Trumpet stand, Bucket, (front, left to right) Straight, Eraser, Pencil, Harmon, Plunger

 MIC TECHNIQUE

When doing live work, you may need to use a microphone. Here are a few things to remember:

- Play in the same way that you would if the microphone wasn't there. If you play with a weak, unsupported sound, that's what will get amplified.

- Position the stand and microphone so that you can play with a good posture and still see the music.

- Unless you're on a very high profile gig, you will be supplied with a Shure 57 or 58 microphone, or something similar. The ideal distance that your bell should be from the mic is about 12 inches (if using a Harmon mute, move in closer). If you get too close, there will be a bass boost and you will lose some sparkle from your sound.

- If you accidently knock the mic stand, it can "boom" quite loudly. If your sound engineer doesn't automatically do so, ask them to apply a low-cut on your mic. This will eliminate the problem and also avoid spill from other low frequencies that might be picked up (the trumpet's range doesn't contain these frequencies, so removing it will not alter your sound). For more detail on frequencies that affect the trumpet's sound, see Tip 53.

 EQ

EQ is the abbreviation of equalization. Most sound engineers have a good knowledge of what the vocals, guitars, bass, drums, and keyboards should sound like, but they may be less used to dealing with brass instruments. It's a good idea to locate the sound engineer when you arrive at a gig so that communication will be easier later on. Ideally, an engineer will come over to listen to your sound to make sure that they are representing it correctly in the front-of-house speakers. If your sound is not quite as you'd like it, you could diplomatically make some suggestions for improvement. First, we need a quick science lecture.

Here are the fundamental frequencies of some different pitches on a B♭ trumpet (the fundamental is the note you are playing. Notice that the frequency is doubled when an octave higher). The exact frequencies have been rounded up here.

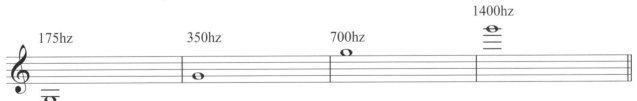

Each of these notes will contain other harmonics (overtones)—which are higher frequencies (up to 15 kHz)—although these are not perceived as actual notes to the listener. Which and how loud these harmonics are will determine a player's tone or timbre (i.e., if you have a very bright tone, there will be many high overtones present and they will be at a greater volume than someone with a dull tone).

If you are basically happy with the sound, but want to improve it slightly, then the rule is to cut (reduce) a frequency. If you want a completely different sound, then boost (increase) a frequency. Here are some guidelines that may help:

Warmth: boost at 200–400 Hz

Nasal/Tinny/Telephone-like: cut at 1–2 kHz

Muddy: cut at 3–4 kHz

Attack: cut or boost at 5 kHz

Rasp/Sizzle: boost at 6–8 kHz

Shrillness: boost at 8–12 kHz

54 MONITOR MIX

Once you have the perfect trumpet sound, you need to think about what you want to hear in your monitor. In general, keep it as quiet as possible, while still being able to hear what you need to. If we take a standard backline (one or two guitars, bass, and drums), vocals, and a brass section, you'll first want your own sound coming back at you. Don't have this overly loud, or you may start to play in a different way to compensate. Next, add the other instruments in from your section so that you hear a good balance.

What else you add in will depend on the size of the stage and how spread out everyone is, how loud the other instruments are, and what type of music you are playing. In general, "less is more"; ask for as few instruments in the monitor as possible. In most cases, I would always add the hi-hat. This will provide you with a fast rhythmic element (usually sixteenth notes) and is at a frequency that is high enough not to interfere with the brass section's sound. If the bass is far away or not very audible, I would add a little of that to help with tuning. You could have everything else in there as well, but for the most part, vocals and guitars will be very prominent in the front-of-house mix, so you probably won't need to hear them in your monitor. It's very rare that you will struggle to hear what the drummer is doing, so percussion can stay out of the mix as well!

Sound travels past listening position

Sound reaches listening position

Wedge-shaped monitors are highly directional, meaning that the speaker should be pointing at your head. If you are standing too close to the monitor, the angle will be wrong.

55 USE A MIRROR

If possible, make sure that you have a long mirror in the room that you use for practicing. In this way, you can check that your posture is correct and that your embouchure is working evenly. If it looks wrong, chances are, it is wrong.

56 TAKE OFF THE PRESSURE

Some people talk about the "no pressure method," but this doesn't exist. You have to apply a certain amount of pressure to the embouchure to make a good seal between the lips and mouthpiece. However, to play with flexibility and endurance, you need to use as little mouthpiece pressure as possible. Everyone will use a little extra pressure towards the end of a tiring gig, but for 99% of the time, you want to be thinking about minimizing it. Some players will find that they use too much pressure all of the time, even on notes that require little effort. What can we do to fix this? Consider the following points:

What does using a small amount of pressure feel like?

Place the tip of your left thumb under the flared bell section and the tip of your right thumb under the lead pipe. You should be able to balance your trumpet quite well. Now play some mid-register long notes. Your embouchure will be doing all the work here, as you won't be able to get any purchase on your instrument to add pressure onto your lips.

How much pressure do I need?

Play a long G in the staff and gradually move the trumpet away from you. At some point, the note will begin to splutter. Just before that point is the amount of pressure you currently need to produce that note. Try the same exercise on a few slightly higher notes. When you're playing, ask yourself, "Do I need this amount of pressure? Could I ease it off a bit?"

What else can I do?

Another thing to do is remove your right-hand little finger from the finger hook (see Tip 74). That will eradicate one of the main culprits for adding mouthpiece pressure.

57 BE CREATIVE

When you start doing professional engagements, you will come across particular phrases or sections that are tricky. Without a teacher around, you need to be able to work out a way to tackle them.

Take this next example:

The hardest part of this phrase is undoubtedly being able to go from A to G♯ cleanly. The traditional approach would be to slow it down, and then gradually build up the tempo—this, of course, will work well and is sound advice. However, to make practicing more focused and productive, get creative:

Try this next example. The tempo is slower, I have altered the rhythm, and added some slurs and accents.

The hardest part of the phrase is now isolated and tackled from a different angle. The accents help to focus on making sure the valves are put down firmly. You may realize that although the tempo is slower, you now have longer to prepare for the G♯ than before. Also the change from the G♯ back to the A is now quicker. Let's try switching the emphasis to the other way around.

Ok, now we're getting somewhere! Let's drop the slurs, but play both versions softly.

Let's add a dynamic change into the mix.

By concentrating on the dynamics, you are asking your subconscious mind to take care of the finger work.

Finally, go back to the original version. You should find that you can play this with much more control and accuracy than before.

This approach can also be used with slurs, tricky intervals, articulation, etc. Hopefully these exercises will show that through creative problem solving, you can make your practice sessions more productive by concentrating on an isolated issue for longer, while also practicing other useful elements.

58 TURN ON THE RED LIGHT

It can be difficult to be completely objective about your own playing, and it is easy to miss certain flaws while you are concentrating on other aspects. You may not be hearing yourself in the same way others do (like if you hear your voice played back on a video clip; it probably sounds different than what you think it does). The way around this is to record your practice and/or gigs. You can do this with a relatively inexpensive handheld digital recorder. The advantage of recording your practice sessions is that you simulate the added pressure of being on a gig—it's as if someone else is listening.

 59 LOOK AT THE RIGHT HAND

When working on scales or a passage that needs some attention in getting the fingers properly synchronized, always look at your right hand. This will focus your concentration fully on the job at hand (no pun intended!).

 60 AVOIDING CRACKED NOTES

A cracked note ("frak," "splinter," "chip," "split," etc.) occurs when you are vibrating the lips at the wrong speed for the intended pitch. This may be because you are not hearing the correct note (see Tip 44), or because your lips are too tired. Cracked notes can affect a player's confidence, but you are likely to be more bothered about it than anyone else is.

Let's do the math. If you played a five-minute piece written at 120 b.p.m., and you crack the first note, a quarter note, the crack would last for just 0.16% of the piece. If you then think about it for the other 99.84% of the time, chances are that you won't be concentrating fully or "keeping in the moment" (see Tip 77), resulting in more cracks.

Even the most famous players occasionally "knock one over," the trick is that they recover from it very quickly and don't let it affect the rest of the performance. In fact, you can hear the occasional crack on some of the most well-known '70s disco tracks. They actually add an energy and feeling of excitement, but that doesn't mean you should try to incorporate them as an effect!

One of the most likely times for a crack to happen is when you are thinking about playing a high note or on an exposed entry. If you think (and therefore hear) that you are going to crack it, you probably will. Instead, hear that note being played beautifully, with a huge sound.

 61 MAKING A LIVING

Especially at the start of your career, it can be hard to achieve a steady income from playing alone. Even when you are more established, there will inevitably be times when work is hard to find. Many of the most successful players supplement their playing income from other sources (often teaching master classes or at a conservatory). Here are some ideas for other avenues to pursue that will hopefully improve the health of your bank balance. They will also help you to develop as a musician, and could be an alternative route into playing work.

- Start your own groups (brass quintet, function band, etc.)
- Approach some churches and offer your skills for weddings and other services
- Play at nursing homes (perhaps some '30s and '40s sing-alongs with a backing track)
- Studios and event organizers – find as many as you can and send a well-polished audio demo and résumé

- Music jobs websites (some interesting things crop up on these)
- Music editing
- Conducting
- Arranging
- Music theory tutoring
- Music copying
- Music production
- Sound engineering
- Teaching – the most constant of incomes. It can be very rewarding and you may be able to coach some ensembles

 ORCHESTRAL EXCERPTS

A good way to learn some of the orchestral repertoire is through excerpt books. Remember that most of what is in them is there for a good reason; it's difficult in some way! Don't get disheartened if you can't play the book from cover to cover. Excerpts are great for transposition practice, covering many different trumpet keys. The downside to these books is that they don't show you the excerpt in context—what is happening in the piece before and after the excerpt, or what the other instruments are doing. To rectify this, always listen to a recording of the work.

A fun way to approach excerpts is to get together with a couple of friends, as there are often parts for three or four trumpets written. In this way you can share ideas on the best way to play them, and work on your tuning and section balance.

 DUETS

Practicing on your own is, of course, something we all need to devote time to on an ongoing basis, but it is not the only way to practice. Practicing duets with another player is hugely beneficial, as you will be working on areas of your playing that you can't (or sometimes neglect) when playing alone. Here are some selling points for duet playing:

- It's fun.
- By listening, you develop your tuning, balance, and ability to match articulations.
- Your sight-reading gets better, as you are more focused on getting it right the first time so that you don't have to keep stopping.
- Your sense of time improves, as you need to keep a strong internal pulse going.
- You learn how to play in a section by following or leading the other player, breathing together, and ending notes at the same time.
- You can learn techniques and musical ideas from another player.
- You will be inspired to play the best you possibly can.

One of the most challenging and satisfying books I have found is the *Artistic Duets for Trumpet*, by Ernest S. Williams.

64 INTERPRETING THE PART

Not everything notated for the trumpet has been written by a trumpet player. If written by an inexperienced arranger or non-wind player, they can often forget that you need to breathe, or be unaware of the physical and technical demands required to play the trumpet. Also, the passage may be beyond your abilities at a given time. So, how can you get around this? Well, your first port of call is to think about what the other trumpet players in your section are doing at that moment. Can one of them cover the long, high note before your exposed solo? If not, then you may have to think a little more creatively:

- If you have a difficult slur over a wide interval, you could use a very soft tongue to make sure that the note speaks properly.

- If you have a series of very long notes without a place to breathe, you could snatch a breath at the end of a phrase (which means that you will cut a note slightly shorter than written).

- Could you play the passage on a smaller trumpet (E♭ or piccolo trumpet)?

- If any other instrument plays the same note, could you leave it out entirely?

- If the passage is beyond your range, you could play it down an octave.

- Would adding or removing a slur between two notes make things easier?

- If you played it softer or louder, would that help?

- Would an alternate fingering make things easier (see Tip 31)?

65 MARKING UP A PART

Some scores have useful information included to help you keep your place and make your job easier, others do not. Add your own cue markings by noting the most obvious things happening—like where there is a definite change in instrumentation, a solo, page turns, or directions from the conductor.

Below, the cues are written in boxes. From these we can see that the conductor is conducting in 2, rather than 4, and at letter A there is an oboe solo. At letter B, the conductor is going to take it slightly faster (the specs symbol reminds you to look at the conductor). At the start of the second staff, there is a note to make sure that you have your mute ready for the next entry. At letter C, the gong cue should prick up your ears and make you focus on counting. Just to confirm that you have your counting correct, there is a marking to tell you that at bar 31 of letter C, listen for the trombone entrance. The final marking lets you know there is plenty of time to turn the page.

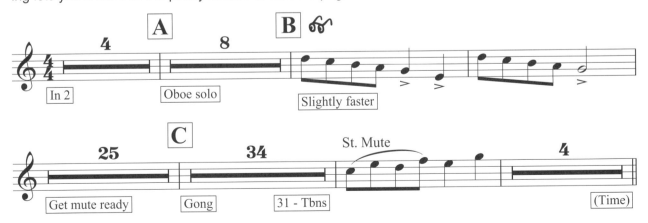

Adding these markings is not only helpful for you, but it will greatly aid anyone coming in to read the part for the first time, i.e., if you hire an engagement out to someone.

66 NOTE FUNCTION

Music has broadly three elements: rhythm, harmony, and melody. By using these in various ways, different emotions are expressed. How you play a note in the context of a piece can contribute to this. Although a note can be a combination of all three elements, it can be useful to ascertain what its prime function is.

Rhythmic

In this example, you can clearly see that there is a strong rhythmic element. This kind of part gives impetus and energy to a piece.

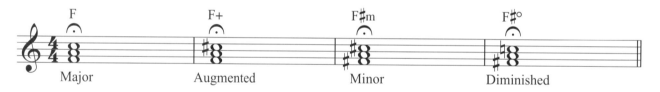

Harmonic

In all of the next examples, I will be referring to the note A. Notice that it serves a different purpose in each chord, depending on the other notes involved. With a thorough understanding of music harmony, and by learning to recognize these different chords aurally, you will have a better idea of what role a note is performing.

The 3rd of a chord is responsible for its quality (major, minor, etc.), and so should be played with a degree of confidence (any hesitance will make the chord sound weak). First, the note A is acting as a major 3rd (major or augmented chord), then as a minor 3rd (minor or diminished chord).

In the next set of chords, the A acts as a suspended 4th, then a suspended 2nd (both of which resolve). Then it acts as a leading note (which is resolved), and finally as a dissonant, cluster type of sound.

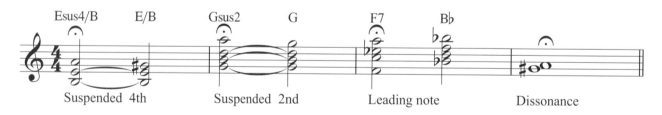

The upper extensions of a chord are usually written for the more prominent, higher-pitched instruments. This is why the trumpet regularly receives these more "exotic" notes to play. Here, the A is acting as the 11th of the E11 chord.

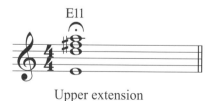

There are many other note functions, such as various 7ths, flattened 9ths, sharpened 11ths, etc., which you could learn to spot by playing them on a piano.

Melodic

Decide whether your part is the main melody or a counter-melody. Broadly speaking, a counter-melody is not the most prominent voice and may be a moving, inner harmony line at a lower pitch, or it may be echoing the main tune (there are many exceptions to this). A counter-melody should complement and not compete with the main melody.

If you play commercial music, there may be occasions when you are tempted to play a phrase or note up an octave. This can be effective, but consider the following points carefully first:

- Does playing it up an octave add anything to the performance, or does it draw attention away from another element (like a vocalist, soloist, or soli section)?
- Will it sound good, or am I likely to crack it?
- By playing this phrase up an octave, am I going to mess up my next entry?
- Is there another note in the higher register coming up that is a climax to a phrase? Will I be making that section less effective?
- Is it in good taste, or am I just show-boating?

One of the hardest things to do on a trumpet is to play an exposed entry, especially after a long rest. Here are a couple of ideas to improve playing a "pearly" entry.

Firstly, hear the notes (see Tip 44). Secondly, relax. If you played this same entry at home, you won't have an issue. If you are worrying about it while counting 48 bars rest, it will be tricky to stay "in the moment" (see Tip 77).

It can be a good idea to practice material not originally intended for the trumpet. In this way, you will have access to music that is more challenging. It may contain phrases that have awkward fingerings, large intervals, notes in the higher register, and phrasing not idiomatic to the trumpet. You could try flute, violin, or saxophone books, but an oboe book is a good option to look at, as the oboe has a range that is fairly similar to that of the trumpet.

 70 FOCUS ON THE SOLOIST

Whatever group you are playing with, it is always considered polite to focus on the soloist (when you're not playing). If you are not doing this, the chances are that you may draw the audience's attention away from the soloist and onto yourself (especially if you are talking to the person next to you). The other reason for concentrating on the soloist is there is always something that you can learn from them. You can observe their breathing, posture, stage presence, phrasing, etc.

 71 LESS IS MORE

When starting out in the world of jazz and improvisation, most players feel a need to fill every available space with sixteenth-notes and technical wizardry. By the time a jazz soloist has crafted their skill, they come to the realization that this isn't what makes for a good solo, and they end up just playing the notes that they feel. If you can find the confidence to approach jazz in this way from the outset, most audience members will believe that you are an accomplished improviser. Something like the last example of the blues solo (Tip 43), shows the use of space and strong musical ideas.

 72 BE PREPARED

As a trumpet player you can be asked to play in a wide variety of styles. If you are about to play a piece or a show that you haven't seen before, never be afraid to ask for the music in advance. As well as being able to practice any tricky parts, you may realize that a piccolo trumpet would be useful, or that you should borrow an unusual mute from a friend. It may not always be possible to get the music early, but people will always be impressed by your conscientiousness.

 73 THE LOUD RIGHT HAND

When playing softly or slowly, the right hand tends to place the valves down more gently or slowly. This results in the starts and transitions of notes sounding unclear. The simple remedy is, when playing softly or slowly, ensure that the right-hand fingers are "playing" loudly (in the same positive manner that you would for a loud section).

74 LITTLE FINGER HOOK

On the very first lesson, most teachers instruct their students to place three fingers over the valve buttons, and their right-hand little finger in the finger hook, which keeps them in the correct position—all well and good. As students try to play higher and higher notes, the likelihood is that they will try to achieve this by using the little finger to pull the trumpet into the lips. As discussed in Tip 56, this is counter-productive. So why is the hook there then? If we think back to the golden age of big bands, the bandleader was often a trumpet player. By using the little finger hook, they could hold and play the trumpet while conducting.

These days, it's not completely redundant, because it is useful when doing a quick mute change, page turn, or some other necessary adjustment. But for the most part, I would avoid using it, and simply rest the little finger on top of the hook. Another advantage of not using the hook is that it frees up the third finger, since it shares a tendon with the little finger.

75 HORN SECTION PLAYING

A "horn section" refers to the brass section of a pop/modern music group, rather than a French horn section of an orchestra. A standard line-up would include trumpet, tenor sax, and trombone; although they can be larger or smaller and may include the alto or baritone sax, and another trumpet or flute.

When playing in a horn section, follow the same rules as when playing in a group as discussed in Tip 37. Some sax players use the pads of the sax to articulate the notes, rather than the tongue. Generally, you want the section to produce a tight, crisp sound, so you may have to subtly remind the sax player to use their tongue.

76 WRITING HORN PARTS

When it comes to writing for the horn section, Jerry Hey is as good as it gets, and it's no wonder so many artists have asked him to add some magic to their tunes. Some of his writing credits include Al Jarreau, Earth, Wind & Fire, Michael Jackson, Average White Band, Jermaine Jackson, Rufus and Chaka Khan, Quincy Jones, Sister Sledge, Michael McDonald, Donna Summer, Diana Ross, George Benson, Nik Kershaw, the Commodores, Whitney Houston, Roberta Flack, Randy Crawford, Lisa Stansfield, Spyro Gyra, Elton John, Arturo Sandoval, Michael Bublé, Queen Latifah, the Pussycat Dolls, and Seal, to name but a few!

If you are interested in writing brass parts, then check out some of these horn sections:

- JB Horns (James Brown)
- The Memphis Horns (soul section who recorded with Isaac Hayes, Otis Redding, Sam & Dave)
- The Phenix Horns (Earth, Wind & Fire and Phil Collins)
- The Tower of Power Horns
- Randy and Michael Brecker

Also worth a listen are these artists who feature horn sections:

- Al Jarreau
- Average White Band
- Bill Chase
- Blood, Sweat & Tears
- Chicago
- Michael Jackson (*Off the Wall*)
- Odyssey
- Rose Royce
- Steely Dan
- Stevie Wonder
- Anything from the Motown or disco era

To be as adept at writing as Jerry Hey takes years of hard work and skill. A good starting point is to transcribe a track that you like and work out what's going on. Depending on the style and what else is happening in the song, the brass section takes on a variety of roles. Here are some of the features and techniques used:

- **Articulation** – parts are often played with precise articulations
- **Complex lines that fit under the vocal** – one of the most difficult things to do, without being too busy
- **Excitement** – brass is used to add an extra dimension or "lift" a song section
- **Falls** – a common technique
- **Filling the gaps** – the most common use of a horn section (sometimes an extension of the main vocal melody)
- **Hooks** – a strong brass riff can "make" a song, think of "Walking on Sunshine" by Katrina and the Waves
- **Intro/outros** – brass can add a powerful beginning or ending to a song
- **Linking sections** – sometimes a middle eight will be played by the brass section to lead to another part of the song
- **Octaves** – brass playing in octaves is powerful and punchy
- **Ostinatos** – most of James Brown's tracks feature a short, repeated phrase
- **Padding** – sometimes a softer approach can be used on longer notes
- **Punctuation** – gaps are often filled with stabs that punctuate a vocal line
- **Riffs** – longer phrases can be repeated such as in "Hold On, I'm Comin'" (Sam & Dave), "Get up Offa That Thing" (James Brown)
- **Runs** – a common feature
- **Sax solos** – more common than trumpet solos
- **Stabs with drums** – usually the drums will catch any stabs that the brass section is doing, for a greater impact
- **Swells** – common on long notes, to add interest
- **Syncopated** – a common technique, sometimes on a monotone

Unless there is a large budget, many of the brass sections that you'll be playing in will consist of just trumpet and tenor sax. Let's look at the last chorus of the blues solo (Tip 43) and use that as the main melody line (this will simulate a vocal line).

For the most part, the horn parts are arranged in octaves or 6ths, as these produce a strong sound for two players.

In the following examples, you will see the trumpet and tenor part (which will sound an octave lower than written), and the guitar line (for the sake of making the harmony clearer to understand, this part is written in the trumpet key). For each version, there is a demo track and a track with the trumpet part removed, so that you can play along with the sax. There is also a backing track, which has no brass at all.

This first version is fairly sparse and could be what you would write for the early part of a song.

- In bar 3, the chromatic figure, which is in octaves, echoes the end of bar 1 of the guitar part.
- In bar 6, the brass dovetails with the last note of the guitar part with some harmony, mostly in 6ths (the sax part is only chromatic from the second note, so that it fits better).
- Then the chromatic pickup of bar 3 happens again, twice.
- Bars 9 and 10 return to more harmony (in 6ths), with some swells.
- Bar 12 sets up the next verse with a chromatic figure in 6ths featuring a shake, then a fall.

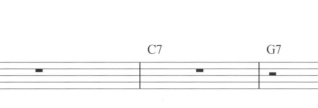

TRACK 63
Demonstration

TRACK 64
Sax with Backing

TRACK 65
Backing Only

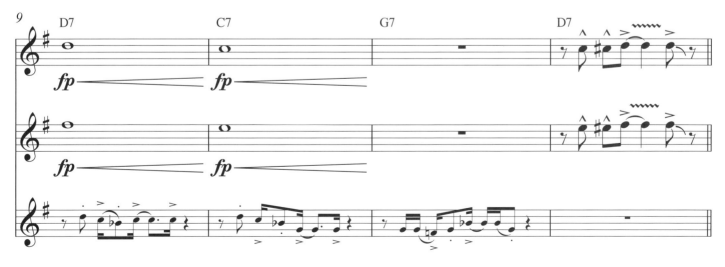

The second version is much busier and would work well on the last chorus of a song.

- In bar 1, there is a "stab" in the space immediately after the first guitar phrase, followed by two more with falls (all in octaves).

- The chromatic figure returns in bar 3, with a C7 figure at the end of bar 4.

- Bar 5 echoes bar 1.

- Bar 6 is similar to the last version, except this time the sax line has been extended.

- Bars 7 and 8 are as before.

- Bar 9 keeps the swell idea in 6ths, but the notes are higher choices. The last three notes dovetail with the end of the guitar part and lead to a stab at the start of bar 10.

- In bar 12, there is a similar idea to the first version, with the C7 figure from bar 4 added.

TRACK 66
Demonstration

TRACK 67
Sax with Backing

TRACK 68
Backing Only

I hope that this tip has given you some ideas to think about. Listen to the demo versions and play along with the sax-only versions, then try to make up your own parts using the backing track (it lasts for 48 bars).

TRACK 69
Backing Track – 48 bars

 # IN THE MOMENT

From time to time, we all get a bit nervous when playing. This is quite normal and can provide an energy that we can use to pull off a stunning performance. Unfortunately, if too severe, your nerves can affect your breathing, which can be a problem. A method that has worked well for me is an approach that keeps you "in the moment."

As an example, imagine that you are playing in an orchestra and you have a tricky solo coming up after 144 bars of rest. If you start worrying about it from the 1st bar, by the time you get to the 144th, you could be very nervous and your breathing is likely to be uncontrollable.

Now, imagine that you are back at the 1st bar of the rest. This time, you are concentrating on everything else going on around you. First, there's an oboe solo—what a great sound she's making, incredible phrasing! Moments later there is a trombone choral; you notice the exquisite tuning and balance within the section. Next, the upper strings play a fast passage with some well-articulated bowing. They are playing as one! Ok, now you have three bars rest to count and it's your solo. You play your solo well, very well in fact! Good job!

By concentrating on other musical events around you, you will pay less attention to your nervousness, which will begin to dissipate. You stay in the moment instead of thinking about an event 144 bars ahead. A book that explores this at great length is the *The Inner Game of Music* by Barry Green, which I believe all musicians should read, whether they are having these sorts of issues or not, as it covers many other aspects of playing and performing.

 SELL YOURSELF

Imagine that you are being asked to do a gig by someone that you don't know. They may ask the rather subjective question, "How good are you?" There is a danger that you may compare yourself to the greats like Maurice André or Cat Anderson, in which case you may not answer very positively! Also, some trumpet players tend to be modest or self-deprecating; this is not what's needed in this situation! What they are actually asking you is, "Are you good enough to do this particular job?" Answer this by talking about what you have done recently and ask for specifics on what's involved for the gig. In that way, you should be able to sell yourself and assure the person that you can handle it.

 FINDING YOUR OWN WAY

Imitation is the highest form of flattery and is the way in which most of us progress as trumpet players. It's a good approach to emulate the best players around you, or ones that you have heard—absorbing their sense of style, use of vibrato, or precise articulation. However, to develop as an individual performer you will need to find the confidence to explore your own ideas. Trusting in the fact that you have a solid technique and have experienced a wealth of musical material, you should have the self-assurance to phrase or articulate passages in your own way. Traits that you admire in other players will remain, but you will be able to offer more of yourself to a performance.

 STYLE

One of the benefits of being a trumpet player is that you can play with many different types of groups, crossing many musical genres. One day you could be rehearsing with an orchestra and the next, recording some horn parts for a pop track. To be able to move in and out of these styles easily, you will need to spend some time finding out about them. To do this, try to join as many different groups as you can. For example, get involved with a local orchestra, jazz, funk, blues, or soca band. You don't have to be involved with a group for very long to enhance your musical knowledge. Then you will be able to approach different styles with a degree of confidence and authenticity.

 TAKE THE OPPORTUNITY

Especially in the early stages of your career, you should take every opportunity that comes your way even if it doesn't seem worthwhile at first. There are many reasons for this including networking possibilities (see Tip 84)—you never know who else will be on the gig. It could be that there is an opportunity to improvise in a low-pressure environment. Also, you can always learn something, whether it be from another player, or a style that you are not familiar with, or at the very least, you will be able to improve your sight-reading.

82 HOW TO PRACTICE

It is possible to practice for hours on end each day and see little improvement. What and how you practice is more important than for how long. How long you practice will depend on the level you are at, and your other commitments. To get the most out of your practice sessions you will need to be organized, disciplined, and methodical.

Organization

Set out a schedule that you can stick to, outlining what you would like to learn or improve. Make sure that there are long, medium, and short-terms goals. For example:

- **12 months** – increase range by a 3rd
- **6 months** – learn to play a blues solo in 12 keys
- **1 week** – transcribe a section of a Tower of Power tune and work on playing it; lip flexibility exercises; long-tone exercises; tricky passages for the concert on Saturday

Each day, make sure that you include a warm-up, technical studies, and some solo pieces of music that you are shortly going to perform. Especially in the warm-up section, make sure that you introduce some variety as boredom can set in if your concentration wanders. To keep focused, include some aspects of other "work in progress." For example, if you are finding out about the jazz modes, you could choose a different mode each day and use it on long-note exercises. In this way you will be using your time very efficiently.

Discipline

Make a commitment to yourself that you will practice every day, rain or shine. There are, of course, times when you will not feel like practicing—just do it anyway! By the time you are a few minutes into practicing, you will find yourself enjoying it and your mood will have lifted.

If possible, make your practice session the first thing you do (after breakfast!); if you leave it until later, the chances are that you will be less motivated and it won't get done.

There is a simple equation: **Consistent Playing = Consistent Practice**

Having a Method

As well as the schedule above, make sure that you are not continually playing.

- At some point, do some practice that doesn't require the trumpet, or actually blowing (see Tip 50).
- Allow some time for listening.
- Build in some breaks, go and make a drink, then return with more focus.
- Balance – if you've been practicing in the higher register, follow it with some low range work. If you've been working in sharp keys, follow it with some work in the flat keys.

Another "trick" is to simulate a problem that you are struggling with. For example, if you are finding it difficult to come in on an entry after a long rest, leave your trumpet out on the side somewhere, pick it up each time you pass, and play the entry cold. This will help you gain the ability to "switch on" at a moment's notice.

83 MENTAL ATTITUDE

Much of trumpet playing is a question of having the right mental attitude. Many of the elements below have been discussed in this book:

- Approach to learning
- Being realistic about time management
- High register development
- Improvising
- Playing in a group
- Overcoming nerves

Another wider concept is having the right attitude when performing in a situation that stretches you. Many would say "play it safe," and there are times when that could be the smart thing to do; it's a judgement call. But some players always play safe. In my opinion, that can lead to a very dull performance and one lacking in expression, excitement, or panache. I would much rather hear someone "going for broke" and giving their all (and missing the odd note), than someone playing the notes that are on the page, but giving nothing of themselves.

84 NETWORKING

With any business, there is a degree of advertising that needs to take place for it to be successful. When you are a freelance trumpet player, you are effectively a business with one employee (i.e., you!). That means that you will need to self-advertise. To be fresh in someone's mind, there are many things that you can do and some preparations to have in place:

- **Be sociable** – at a rehearsal or gig, be friendly and interested in the other musicians; no one wants to spend time with someone who is always miserable.
- **Demos** – prepare a well-polished sample of your best performances and send it to as many studios and event organizers as you can.
- **Cards** – a business card, although low-tech, is a very convenient way to pass on your contact details.
- **Right place, right time** – go to lots of gigs, here you will meet other musicians who may be out of your regular circle.
- **Social networking sites** – there are quite a few of these around and some players have found them to be a useful tool.

85 GET ME TO THE GIG ON TIME

There are very few excuses that are ever acceptable for showing up to a gig or rehearsal late. If you are late, as well as being disruptive for the other musicians, you probably will not be focused or playing at your best. If you get a reputation for being late, it can be very difficult to shake and will affect the number of gigs that you are offered.

It is much better to be an hour early and have the time to relax with a coffee and be able to chat with other players than get to the gig with seconds to spare. The simple message is: get organized!

- Get everything ready in advance: clothes, music, mutes, music stand, etc.
- Don't plan to get there on time, plan to be early.
- If travelling by bus or train, check the times in advance and get an earlier departure than needed.
- If travelling by car, check the map and know where you're going. Don't put all your faith in the GPS; check travel websites for road construction; leave extra time for possible delays.
- If carpooling, don't agree to someone else's timetable if they are not willing to leave enough time.
- If a gig is likely to be very stressful, make the journey as easy as possible. You could even rehearse the journey the day before, if you have the time and it's not too far away. Make sure that you know where you can park your car.

86 FORM YOUR OWN GROUP

Forming your own group can be rewarding in a number of ways. You can hone your arranging skills, be responsible for creating your own work, and come together with like-minded players with whom you can build a bond. Some suggestions are:

- Brass quintet
- Small jazz ensemble
- Function band (cover band for weddings, parties, etc.)
- Original pop band (including funk, soul, blues, etc.)
- Concert band, big band, or orchestra—although these require a great deal of organization

Choose material that everyone will enjoy, that way you are more likely to keep the group together. Finding a suitable rehearsal space can take some time, but there are some suggestions in Tip 40. Get a demo produced and any suitable promotional materials (business cards, website, and branding if appropriate). Contact as many event organizers and agents as you can find—good luck!

 THE FLUGEL

The flugelhorn is a great instrument that many trumpet players "double" on. It produces a warmer sound than the trumpet and is typically used in jazz, commercial, and brass band music, often with featured solos.

The flugel has a wider bore and is conical (gets continuously larger, unlike the trumpet, which only starts to get larger after the 1st valve). This results in less resistance and requires less effort to play, but this can vary enormously from make to make, so try as many as you can before buying one. Tuning can be more of an issue than on the trumpet, although some makes and models fair better than others do.

You will need a dedicated flugel mouthpiece. Even if your trumpet mouthpiece fits, it will not create the correct sound. I would recommend choosing a similar rim to that of your trumpet mouthpiece.

 LEARNING FROM OTHERS

The art of playing the trumpet is an ongoing process and even the top professionals strive to improve their abilities. You will find out many things for yourself; when you are practicing you may have the odd "eureka" moment (they can happen!). What's equally important is to be open to the idea of learning from others. Every player is unique and finds certain things easier to do than others. By watching gigs, listening to recordings, and discussing with others, you will have a greater insight into how to approach problems that you may be working on.

If you are the least experienced member of a group, you have the potential to learn the most. Although this can be a little intimidating, if you are aware and soak up everything that's going on around you, you won't be the least experienced for long.

Don't solely limit yourself to trumpet players or a genre that you commonly work in—singers and other musicians can offer further insights. For example, listen to the vocal phrasing of Frank Sinatra, or a guitar solo by Mark Knopfler.

 REHEARSAL BANDS

Rehearsal bands or reading bands (bands which get together just to play music, rather than for a gig) are a good place for like-minded musicians to meet and enjoy playing. If you don't have too many gigs, they are a great way to help you stay "match-fit" (as you have to play at louder volumes than you might at home). As an added bonus, they are an excellent setting for networking. If you don't have one in your local area, you could ask a few players you know if they would like to help you put one together. In that way, it will spread the organizational load.

SIGHT-READING

One of the most overlooked elements of progressing as a trumpet player is improving your sight-reading. There are books dedicated to this, which are useful, but just get your hands on as much material as you can. When you're playing something for the first time, you have many things to consider, such as watching the conductor, playing in tune and in time, getting the style correct, phrasing, and of course playing the right notes and rhythms. However, there are certain things that you can do before you start. Think of it as a "pre-flight-check":

- **Keys and key changes** – glance through the music and mentally mark where these are (e.g., we start in E major and at the bottom of page 2, we go to F major).

- **Time signatures and time changes** – a similar process to above, this would also include tempo or style changes.

- **Repeats** – make sure that you have the correct geography of the tune mapped out—where does that repeat go back to? Is there a D.S. or a D.C. and will the repeats count on a D.S.? Is there a coda? Do you need to think about a tricky page turn?

- **Patterns, scales, and arpeggios** – looking for phrases or sequences that keep coming back can save you from reading the same pattern twice. Most music will be derived from scales and/or arpeggios, whether in their entirety or in part. Noting that a phrase has the notes C, C#, D, D#, and E could be thought of as a short chromatic run from C to E; this will save some thinking power when reading.

- *Colla voce* **(follow the speed of the vocalist), pauses, and railroad tracks (*caesura*)** – *Colla voce* sections require you to concentrate a bit harder, paying close attention to the conductor and/or soloist. Pauses and railroad tracks are points to strongly observe, as missing one can be embarrassing.

Have a look through the following example and perform a "pre-flight check":

Hopefully you made the following observations:

- It's in 4/4 time at 120 b.p.m. and eighth notes are swung.
- It starts in A major and goes to E♭ major at measure 6.
- Measure 3 is the same as measure 1; measure 4 is a chromatic run down from C# to F.

- There's a pause in measure 5.
- Measures 6 and 7 have the same pattern as measures 1 and 2, but in the new key.
- Measure 8 uses part of an E♭ major or Cm7 arpeggio.
- The tempo is much faster at measure 9 and eighth notes are played straight.
- Measures 9–11 contain a sequence, which is raised one step each measure.

 VALVE TUNING

Tuning can vary from make to make and model to model, so make sure that you choose a new instrument wisely and know the idiosyncrasies of your particular instrument.

Sharp

The most obviously out-of-tune notes on the trumpet are the low D and C♯, which are sharp, so you need to use the 3rd valve trigger slide to correct this. The lowest G and F♯ are usually fine on most instruments, and won't need adjusting. Some notes played with the 1st and 2nd valves together can also be sharp, such as low E, A in the staff, and A just above the staff. Use the 1st valve trigger slide to flatten these. You may find that playing them with the 3rd valve, instead of valves 1 and 2, works for your instrument.

Flat

Notes using the 2nd and 3rd valves may be slightly flat, as are most using the 1st valve alone. "Lip" these up to the required pitch. Also, E (top space in the staff) is generally flat.

 THE HIGHER REGISTER

The upper register can be a constant concern for many players. To improve this aspect of your playing, you need to bring several concepts together at once. Let's look at each one and combine them with the exercises that follow.

Mental Attitude

- If you are a classical player, you will rarely be required to play above a high D. If you are, it will usually be on a smaller trumpet, which makes the job a little easier. In the commercial music arena, for the most part, the same range will get you a long way. It's only if you want to become a lead trumpet player that you will require a range above that, around the super G area. It's much better to have a fantastic tone and be a little short on range, than to be able to scream up high with an unpleasant sound.

- Many players embark on a life-long quest to find the perfect mouthpiece that allows them to play in the middle and lower registers with a full sound and to play high effortlessly. Sadly, I don't think it exists. A shallow mouthpiece will help with the higher register, but the middle and lower ranges will be virtually unusable. Endurance with a solid technique is the path to enlightenment. There are no short cuts!

- There are many higher register method books available that may work for some. Not all books will be suitable for all players and some will cover just one element of technique.

- Believing that one day you will be able to reach the higher notes is the first preparation that is essential for improvement. The other tool you'll need is the ability to hear what the notes should sound like. Even if the notes aren't sounding as full as you'd like them to, the act of imagining it sounding a different way will help bring all the required elements together.

- Work on the higher register with an expectation that it will be a gradual process and you will do it in a measured way. Do not get disheartened if results do not happen immediately—Rome wasn't built in a day!

Consistency

- This is where most players fall down, as it's the one that requires a long-term commitment. You need to be practicing on a very regular basis for improvement to take place. Increased muscle strength will not happen through practicing an endurance exercise once.

- The action of doing something just beyond your reach repeatedly is what will cause the muscles to build.

- Muscle strength will only increase when your body "thinks" there is a reason to do so. For example, if you do some bicep curls at the gym, on the first day you may manage 10 repetitions; two days later, you may manage 10 again, but they might seem a little easier. On the third visit, you may manage 11, and so on.

Mouthpiece Pressure

- For the lips to vibrate, there needs to be as little mouthpiece pressure as possible. Pushing the mouthpiece onto your lips harder will help you achieve a higher note, but you will not be able to play for long periods in this way, as at some point the mouthpiece will stop the lips from vibrating.

- You may find it helpful to think of actually moving the mouthpiece away from you slightly, the higher you go. This will help to keep the pressure off, and in so doing, encourage the embouchure to do the work.

Air Function

- The role of the air stream is an important one, especially in the higher register. The air needs to be very well supported by the diaphragm and extremely fast in a narrow stream. You already know how to do this—when you sneeze, the diaphragm forces the air out at an incredible rate (the average speed of a sneeze is 90 mph, and some have been recorded at 110mph—the same speed as a category 2 hurricane!).

- When the air is whistling past the lips at this speed, like a focused laser beam, it "excites" only a small area of the lips, which will help enormously in producing higher pitches. To help achieve this, arch your tongue so that the mouth cavity above it is small. In this way you will be producing more of a hissing sound, think "tissssssssss." The tongue should not come forward or between the teeth.

- At the same time, make sure that your throat is open, so that you don't obstruct the air before it gets to the tongue.

Embouchure and Buzz

- Ensure that you have warmed up properly.

- The corners of the embouchure need to be tight in order to clamp the lips together, otherwise the lips will be "blown" apart by the "hissing hurricane" air speed mentioned above. Through endurance exercises you can build up the strength of these muscles.

- The buzz needs to be fast and focused in the center of the lips (aided by the fast air stream).

- Use only one embouchure for the entire range of your instrument. False embouchures will result in limited success and ungraceful transitions between registers.

- When doing endurance exercises, ensure that you rest as much as you play. Make sure this includes pedal tones, as these will get the blood returning to the lips and vibrating well.

- Increased endurance comes from including this type of work into your regular practice regime.

- When playing these types of exercises, continue to play just beyond the point where you feel tired.

- In your practice sessions, plan to have "A" and "B" days, where you include higher register work on the "A" days and work on other aspects on the "B" days. The lips need time to recover and generate muscle growth; this will not happen if you "pound" them every day. If you leave it too long between "A" days (say a week or two), then the new muscle strength will disappear (as the body assumes that it is no longer required).

- If you are too impatient, there is a danger that you will overdo things. Be careful. Don't exert yourself way beyond your limit, as this will hamper what you are able to play the next day. Be aware of when you've gone a bit too far and decide to rein it in next time.

- Always warm down after endurance work with some soft, long, low notes or pedal tones. This will ensure that your lips are responsive for the following day.

Ok, that's a lot of thinking! Now on to an exercise; remember the following:

- Play at the **tempo** marked.

- Make sure that you have **warmed up** properly beforehand.

- **Believe** that you can improve your range.

- Use **minimal mouthpiece pressure**.

- Change the **vowel sound** that your tongue is making as you play up the slur.

- **Increase the air** volume, support, and speed as you play up the slur (**tiss**).

- Make sure that the **throat is open**.

- Use your **normal embouchure** throughout—make the **corner of your lips firmer**, the higher up you go.

- Loosen the lips with **pedal tones**.

- Observe the **rests**.

- Always **work through from the start** of the exercise.

- **Do not over-exert yourself**. Play one arpeggio more than you can currently easily manage.

- Remember, some days will be easier than others; think of the **long-term goal**.

- Make sure that you **warm down**.

In this exercise, the suggested vowel sounds are only a rough guide. You may find that you need to change to a different vowel earlier or later than shown. Bear in mind that you should gradually change from one vowel to another.

TRACK 70

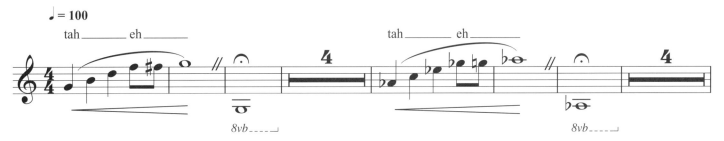

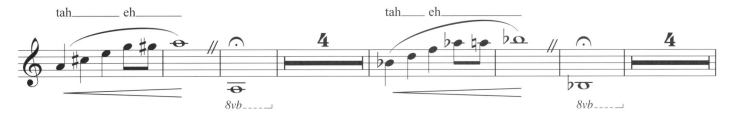

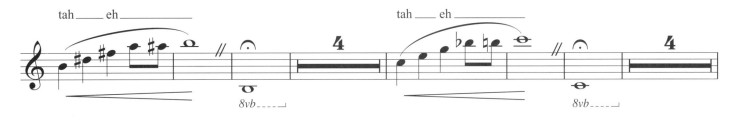

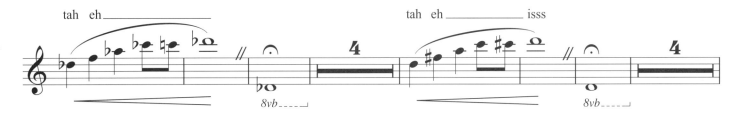

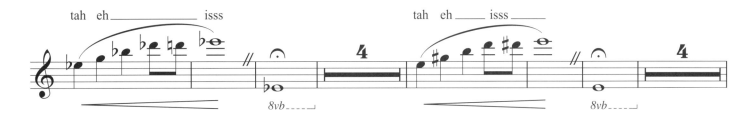

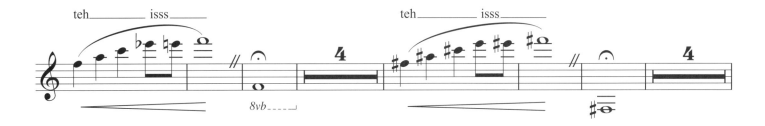

With the following exercises, continue the same pattern upward chromatically, until you reach a point where you start to tire.

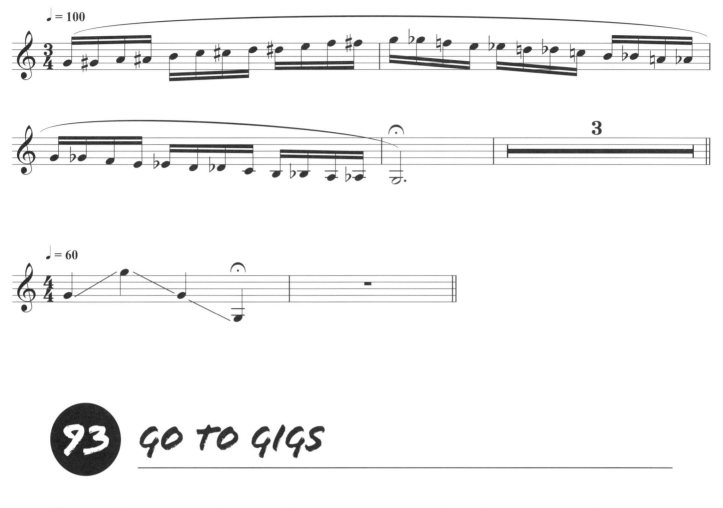

93 GO TO GIGS

When musicians start to get busy, one thing that seems to be neglected is going to watch gigs. As discussed in other tips, it's a great opportunity to learn something. You may pick up all sorts of ideas, sometimes from the more unobvious. For example, you might want to ask the sound engineer how he or she got the trumpet to sound so good. The other reason to go to gigs is that you will enjoy it, probably be inspired to practice harder, and work on other aspects of your playing.

94 PERFECT SOMETHING EVERY DAY

It can be hard to see an immediate improvement in your playing when practicing an advanced technique or working toward a long-term goal (see Tip 97). To maintain morale and keep the bar set high, always try to perfect something every day. It needn't be anything too hard. It could be as simple as playing a new scale pattern in every key or transposing the first four bars of an orchestral excerpt. Doing this will help you to have a sense of achievement when other progress seems slow.

 PUSH YOURSELF

When practicing, don't stick to the things you can already play. It might make you feel good, but it won't help you to progress. Always push yourself to just beyond your present ability. For example, play a note that's out of your current range, improvise over a chord progression that's not familiar to you, or work on a technical aspect that you find difficult. This may seem in contradiction to the previous tip, but a mixture of "harder" and "not so hard" challenges can be a productive approach.

 PLAY-ALONGS

There are countless play-alongs on the market, mostly for jazz players. These can be a very good tool if you use them wisely. As a start, I would suggest working on the blues, II-V-Is, and rhythm changes, as many jazz standards are based on or incorporate these chord progressions.

Once you are happy with the progression, make sure that you tackle the harder keys, as this will improve your confidence in tackling unfamiliar tunes. Find out what tunes are based on these progressions and improvise "on the tune" rather than relying on pre-learned licks. Although licks can sound impressive and are good for learning how to play in an idiom, the true improviser refers to the head (melody) in their solos.

 BE REALISTIC

When you start your practice session, make sure that you have a plan for what you want to achieve that day (see Tip 82), but be realistic. There is no point in thinking, "I'm going to increase my range by a 5th today!"

The most important thing to get right is "what" you want to work on. How long it takes will depend on your concentration levels, what playing you did over the previous days, your motivation, and the difficulty of the goals you have set.

Some improvements can be seen in a matter of minutes, while others are imperceptible changes that are worked on by the subconscious or muscles that are slowly getting stronger. You may only see evidence of these improvements months later, when you return to a piece and find that you can now play the tricky passages with ease. So, make sure that your goals are clear, and accept that some challenges will take minutes and others weeks, months, or years.

 **TONE**

Getting a good tone should be at the top of every musician's list of goals to achieve. Technical brilliance and high notes are nothing without it. You need the right tools for the job; these include a mouthpiece that will allow a full tone to be produced across your entire range (i.e., not one at the extremes of what is available) and a decent quality instrument that is resonant and can project. The rest is up to you!

- **Regular practice** – essential to good tone development.
- **A perception of what a good sound is** – you need to know what you're trying to achieve, so have that in mind at all times. Listen to others, go to gigs, listen to recordings, and record yourself so that you can be objective about what you sound like.
- **Pure buzz** – start with the buzz, as this gets amplified through the instrument (see Tip 6).
- **Equal tone across the entire range** – you don't want to hear a big change in timbre as you go from one note to another. Excellent exercises for this are scales, arpeggios, and long notes.
- **Air supply** – a well-supported airstream means that you will have a buoyant, bright tone. No support results in a sagging, dull tone.

 **RECOVERY**

Trumpet players need to be aware of the physical demands of playing the instrument. Bad technique resulting in too much mouthpiece pressure (see Tip 56) can lead to bruising of the lips. When this happens, the lips will not vibrate properly, which often leads to even more mouthpiece pressure to get any sort of result. Obviously this is bad! If this happens, you can use Arnica cream (an extract from the Arnica plant), which will help to reduce any swelling and promotes tissue healing, but I would also recommend taking a couple of days off. It is better to miss a couple of days practicing than to compound the problem and get frustrated. You could use this time for other practice that doesn't involve the lips (see Tip 50).

 **IT'S ALL RELATIVE**

Dynamics are a set of instructions that can vary enormously. A *fortissimo* written in a big band chart may be much louder than that of a Brahms symphony; dynamics must fit the context of the style and piece. Also, it depends what the instrumentation is at the time. If playing a requiem, for example, the orchestration may suddenly change from a full symphony orchestra with choir, to a chamber-sized ensemble with a solo soprano. The composer may still want a full range of dynamics, albeit on a softer scale.

101 TROUBLESHOOTING

Some of these problems and solutions have been covered or touched on in this book, others are frequently raised issues.

Problem	Cause/Solution
I can't slur cleanly between two notes.	Practice lip flexibilities with vowel change "ah" to "eh." Ensure valve changes are swift, especially during soft passages or at slower tempos.
I can't play high.	Too much mouthpiece pressure, not enough air; work on endurance and consistent practice.
I can't play low.	Mouthpiece may be too small and/or shallow; reduce mouthpiece pressure, lower bottom jaw.
I can't play quietly.	Use fast, narrow air stream with support, reduce mouthpiece pressure, work on buzzing.
My lip gives out before the end of a gig.	Take it easy during a rehearsal, practice regularly, practice with the same volume and projection as needed for the gig, reduce mouthpiece pressure.
My sound is airy.	Listen to other players, concentrate on getting a "pure" buzz with the lips alone, ensure regular practice.
I can't play in tune.	Make sure trumpet is clean inside, get dents removed, match the notes with an electronic piano, use a tuner to monitor.
My articulation is poor.	Mouthpiece may be too shallow; use correct "tu" syllable and correct tongue placement. Ensure fingers and tongue are synchronized.
My tone is thin.	Mouthpiece may be too shallow; ensure you practice consistently.
My tone is dull.	Mouthpiece too deep, lack of proper air support.
Mouthpiece cuts into lips.	Reduce mouthpiece pressure, find a mouthpiece with a rim that is less sharp.
I haven't got time to practice.	Practicing just a short time every day (even ten minutes) is more productive than completing only one long session per week.

Presenting the Hal Leonard JAZZ PLAY-ALONG SERIES

For use with all B-flat, E-flat, Bass Clef and C instruments, the Jazz Play-Along® Series is the ultimate learning tool for all jazz musicians. With musician-friendly lead sheets, melody cues, and other split-track choices on the included CD, these first-of-a-kind packages help you master improvisation while playing some of the greatest tunes of all time. FOR STUDY, each tune includes a split track with: melody cue with proper style and inflection • professional rhythm tracks • choruses for soloing • removable bass part • removable piano part. FOR PERFORMANCE, each tune also has: an additional full stereo accompaniment track (no melody) • additional choruses for soloing.

63. CLASSICAL JAZZ
00843064 .... $14.95

64. TV TUNES
00843065 .... $14.95

65. SMOOTH JAZZ
00843066 .... $16.99

66. A CHARLIE BROWN CHRISTMAS
00843067 .... $16.99

67. CHICK COREA
00843068 .... $15.95

68. CHARLES MINGUS
00843069 .... $16.95

69. CLASSIC JAZZ
00843071 .... $15.99

70. THE DOORS
00843072 .... $14.95

71. COLE PORTER CLASSICS
00843073 .... $14.95

72. CLASSIC JAZZ BALLADS
00843074 .... $15.99

73. JAZZ/BLUES
00843075 .... $14.95

74. BEST JAZZ CLASSICS
00843076 .... $15.99

75. PAUL DESMOND
00843077 .... $14.95

76. BROADWAY JAZZ BALLADS
00843078 .... $15.99

77. JAZZ ON BROADWAY
00843079 .... $15.99

78. STEELY DAN
00843070 .... $14.99

79. MILES DAVIS CLASSICS
00843081 .... $15.99

80. JIMI HENDRIX
00843083 .... $15.99

81. FRANK SINATRA – CLASSICS
00843084 .... $15.99

82. FRANK SINATRA – STANDARDS
00843085 .... $15.99

83. ANDREW LLOYD WEBBER
00843104 .... $14.95

84. BOSSA NOVA CLASSICS
00843105 .... $14.95

85. MOTOWN HITS
00843109 .... $14.95

86. BENNY GOODMAN
00843110 .... $14.95

87. DIXIELAND
00843111 .... $14.95

88. DUKE ELLINGTON FAVORITES
00843112 .... $14.95

89. IRVING BERLIN FAVORITES
00843113 .... $14.95

90. THELONIOUS MONK CLASSICS
00841262 .... $16.99

91. THELONIOUS MONK FAVORITES
00841263 .... $16.99

92. LEONARD BERNSTEIN
00450134 .... $15.99

93. DISNEY FAVORITES
00843142 .... $14.99

94. RAY
00843143 .... $14.99

95. JAZZ AT THE LOUNGE
00843144 .... V$14.99

96. LATIN JAZZ STANDARDS
00843145 .... $14.99

97. MAYBE I'M AMAZED*
00843148 .... $15.99

98. DAVE FRISHBERG
00843149 .... $15.99

99. SWINGING STANDARDS
00843150 .... $14.99

100. LOUIS ARMSTRONG
00740423 .... $15.99

101. BUD POWELL
00843152 .... $14.99

102. JAZZ POP
00843153 .... $14.99

103. ON GREEN DOLPHIN STREET
& OTHER JAZZ CLASSICS
00843154 .... $14.99

104. ELTON JOHN
00843155 .... $14.99

105. SOULFUL JAZZ
00843151 .... $15.99

106. SLO' JAZZ
00843117 .... $14.99

107. MOTOWN CLASSICS
00843116 .... $14.99

108. JAZZ WALTZ
00843159 .... $15.99

109. OSCAR PETERSON
00843160 .... $16.99

110. JUST STANDARDS
00843161 .... $15.99

111. COOL CHRISTMAS
00843162 .... $15.99

112. PAQUITO D'RIVERA – LATIN JAZZ*
48020662 .... $16.99

113. PAQUITO D'RIVERA – BRAZILIAN JAZZ*
48020663 .... $19.99

114. MODERN JAZZ QUARTET FAVORITES
00843163 .... $15.99

115. THE SOUND OF MUSIC
00843164 .... $15.99

116. JACO PASTORIUS
00843165 .... $15.99

117. ANTONIO CARLOS JOBIM – MORE HITS
00843166 .... $15.99

118. BIG JAZZ STANDARDS COLLECTION
00843167 .... $27.50

119. JELLY ROLL MORTON
00843168 .... $15.99

120. J.S. BACH
00843169 .... $15.99

121. DJANGO REINHARDT
00843170 .... $15.99

122. PAUL SIMON
00843182 .... $16.99

123. BACHARACH & DAVID
00843185 .... $15.99

124. JAZZ-ROCK HORN HITS
00843186 .... $15.99

126. COUNT BASIE CLASSICS
00843157 .... $15.99

127. CHUCK MANGIONE
00843188 .... $15.99

132. STAN GETZ ESSENTIALS
00843193 .... $15.99

133. STAN GETZ FAVORITES
00843194 .... $15.99

134. NURSERY RHYMES*
00843196 .... $17.99

135. JEFF BECK
00843197 .... $15.99

136. NAT ADDERLEY
00843198 .... $15.99

137. WES MONTGOMERY
00843199 .... $15.99

138. FREDDIE HUBBARD
00843200 .... $15.99

139. JULIAN "CANNONBALL" ADDERLEY
00843201 .... $15.99

141. BILL EVANS STANDARDS
00843156 .... $15.99

150. JAZZ IMPROV BASICS
00843195 .... $19.99

151. MODERN JAZZ QUARTET CLASSICS
00843209 .... $15.99

157. HYMNS
00843217 .... $15.99

162. BIG CHRISTMAS COLLECTION
00843221 .... $24.99

*These CDs do not include split tracks.

0811

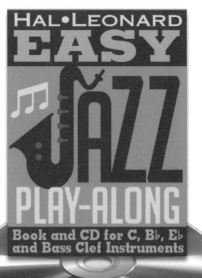

HAL•LEONARD EASY JAZZ PLAY-ALONG

Book and CD for C, B♭, E♭ and Bass Clef Instruments

IMPROVISING IS EASIER THAN EVER

with this new series for beginning jazz musicians. The Hal Leonard Easy Jazz Play-Along Series includes songs with accessible chord changes and features recordings with novice-friendly tempos. Just follow the streamlined lead sheets in the book and play along with the professionally recorded backing tracks on the CD. The bass or piano can also be removed by turning down the volume on the left or right channel. The audio CD is playable on any CD player. For PC and Mac computer users, the CD is enhanced so you can adjust the recording to any tempo without changing pitch!

1. FIRST JAZZ SONGS
Book/CD Pack

All of Me • All the Things You Are • Autumn Leaves • C-Jam Blues • Comin' Home Baby • Footprints • The Girl from Ipanema (Garôta De Ipanema) • Killer Joe • Little Sunflower • Milestones • Mr. P.C. • On Green Dolphin Street • One for Daddy-O • Reunion Blues • Satin Doll • There Will Never Be Another You • Tune Up • Watermelon Man.

00843225 B♭, E♭, C & Bass Clef Instruments..............$19.99

2. STANDARDS FOR STARTERS
Book/CD Pack

Don't Get Around Much Anymore • Exactly like You • Fly Me to the Moon (In Other Words) • Have You Met Miss Jones? • Honeysuckle Rose • I Remember You • If I Should Lose You • It Could Happen to You • Moon River • My Favorite Things • On a Slow Boat to China • Out of Nowhere • Softly As in a Morning Sunrise • Speak Low • The Very Thought of You • Watch What Happens • The Way You Look Tonight • Yesterdays.

00843226 B♭, E♭, C & Bass Clef Instruments..............$19.99

3. VITAL JAZZ CLASSICS
Book/CD Pack

Afternoon in Paris • Doxy • 500 Miles High • Girl Talk • Holy Land • Impressions • In Walked Bud • The Jive Samba • Lady Bird • Maiden Voyage • Mercy, Mercy, Mercy • My Little Suede Shoes • Recorda-Me • St. Thomas • Solar • Song for My Father • Stolen Moments • Sunny.

00843227 B♭, E♭, C & Bass Clef Instruments..............$19.99

4. BASIC BLUES
Book/CD Pack

All Blues • Birk's Works • Bloomdido • Blue Seven • Blue Train (Blue Trane) • Blues in the Closet • Cousin Mary • Freddie Freeloader • The Jody Grind • Jumpin' with Symphony Sid • Nostalgia in Times Square • Now See How You Are • Now's the Time • Sonnymoon for Two • Tenor Madness • Things Ain't What They Used to Be • Turnaround • Two Degrees East, Three Degrees West.

00843228 B♭, E♭, C & Bass Clef Instruments..............$19.99

HAL•LEONARD® CORPORATION

7777 W. BLUEMOUND RD. P.O. BOX 13819 MILWAUKEE, WI 53213

Prices, content, and availability subject to change without notice.

1211